# SPIRITUALITY IN

# SPIRITUALITY IN THE CITY

Edited by Andrew Walker

First published in Great Britain in 2005

Society for Promoting Christian Knowledge
36 Causton Street
London SW1P 4ST

British Library Cataloguing-in-Publication Data
A catalogue record for this book is available from the British Library

ISBN 0–281–05703–6

1 3 5 7 9 10 8 6 4 2

Typeset by Graphicraft Limited, Hong Kong
Printed in Great Britain by Ashford Colour Press

# Contents

# Contributors

**Rosalind Brown** is a Canon Residentiary of Durham Cathedral. Until the summer of 2005 she was a staff member of the Southern Theological Education and Training Scheme, based at Sarum College, Salisbury, and Vice Principal of the Diocese of Salisbury Ordained Local Ministry Scheme. Originally a town planner, she lived for several years in the USA, where she was ordained and was a member of an Episcopal Religious Community. She is the author of *Being a Deacon Today* (Canterbury Press, 2005) and, with Christopher Cocksworth, of *Being a Priest Today* (Canterbury Press, 2002) and *How Hymns Shape Our Lives* (Grove, 2001). Several of her hymn texts have won prizes and have been published on both sides of the Atlantic, most recently with Jeremy Davies and Ron Green in *Sing! New Words for Worship* (Sarum College Press, 2004).

**Andrew Davey** has been a parish priest in Southwark and Peckham. He is currently National Adviser on Community and Urban Affairs to the Archbishops' Council. Author of *Urban Christianity and Global Order* (SPCK, 2001), he is currently writing on the interaction between spirituality and informal urban politics in globalizing cities. He delivered the 2004 Bishop Williams Memorial Lectures at Rikkyo University, Tokyo on *Global Cities and the Future of God*. He lives and cycles in inner London.

**Bernadette Flanagan** is a Roman Catholic religious sister. She has lived and worked in Dublin since 1987. Her first book, *The Spirit of the City: Voices from Dublin's Liberties* (Veritas, 1999), was the fruit of her reflection on interviews with the long-term residents of Dublin's inner city. Since 1999 she has been head of the Department of Spirituality at Milltown Institute, Dublin.

In this position she has been at the forefront of several new initiatives in spirituality in Ireland, designing an MA in Applied Spirituality and an MA in Supervisory Practice for those in the ministry of spiritual accompaniment, organizing and hosting the first European conference to reflect on the academic study of spirituality in Europe (June 2004), and setting in train the movement that established the All Ireland Spiritual Guidance Association (<http://www.aisga.org>). On the occasion of the graduation of the first participants from the MA in Applied Spirituality programme, Bernadette gathered the reflections of some staff and students on the new trends that are emerging in spirituality. This was published in 2004: B. Flanagan, D. Kelly, eds, *Lamplighters: Exploring Spirituality in New Contexts* (Dublin, Veritas).

**Leslie Griffiths** was educated at Llanelli Grammar School before studying for a BA at University College, Cardiff, between 1960 and 1963. He spent a year there as a research fellow before becoming an assistant lecturer in Medieval English at St David's College, Lampeter. He trained at Wesley House, Cambridge for the Methodist ministry and spent much of the 1970s as a minister in Haiti, either in community development work or in education. Since his return to the UK in 1980 he has served the Church in a variety of posts in or around London. Since 1996 he has been superintendent minister at Wesley's Chapel. In 1994–5, he was President of the Methodist Conference. He has been a member of various committees, reflecting his interests in higher education, broadcasting and ecumenical relations. He broadcasts regularly on *Thought for the Day* and *The Daily Service*, and writes for *The Methodist Recorder, The Tablet* and the *Church Times*. He has published five books. In 2004 he was awarded a life peerage. He is married to Margaret and they have three children.

**Clare Herbert** is the Rector of St Anne's Church, in Soho, and the Dean of Women for the Two Cities area of the London diocese. Before taking up this post she was the project director of Websters, a spirituality centre for women on Tottenham Court Road, and a curate at St Martin-in-the-Fields, Trafalgar Square. She came to London 12 years ago from Bristol, where she had been a child and family social worker and a non-stipendiary deacon. Despite growing up in a remote part of Devon, on the northern edge of Dartmoor, as an adult she has lived and worked entirely in cities, and she brings to her work there the strong sense of Church as community that she gained in the country towns and villages of her childhood. Like many of her generation, she has been strongly influenced by the spirituality of Thomas Merton, but has always longed for it to move from beneath the redwood trees to the streets of the towns and cities that shape so many lives.

**Mark Oakley** is Archdeacon of Germany and Northern Europe. Until the summer of 2005 he was Rector of St Paul's, Covent Garden (The Actors' Church), Area Dean of Westminster (St Margaret) and a Deputy Priest in Ordinary to the Queen. He was educated at Shrewsbury, London and Oxford, and was ordained in the Church of England in 1993. He served as Assistant Curate of St John's Wood Church, then as Chaplain to the Bishop of London, before taking up his present appointment. He regularly reviews, broadcasts and lectures on literary and theological topics, and is the author of *The Collage of God* (Darton, Longman and Todd, 2001) and *John Donne: Verse and Prose* (SPCK, 2004).

**Philip Sheldrake** is William Leech Professorial Fellow in Applied Theology at the University of Durham. He was educated at Oxford and London Universities, and trained in modern history, philosophy and theology. He previously taught at London University, Cambridge and Sarum College, Salisbury (in association with the University of Wales Lampeter), and is regularly a visiting professor at North American universities. He has written and edited extensively in the field of

Christian spirituality and is a former President of the international Society for the Study of Christian Spirituality, associated with the American Academy of Religion. Over the past ten years he has increasingly focused his work on place and identity: for example, his book *Spaces For the Sacred: Place, Memory and Identity* (SCM Press/Johns Hopkins University Press, 2001) was based on his 1999 Hulsean Lectures at Cambridge. He is currently involved in interdisciplinary research, writing and lecturing on the meaning of cities and the spiritual/ethical dimensions of city-making and urban living.

**Andrew Walker** was ordained in 1985 and has served in parishes in Fareham, St John's Wood and Streatham. He is currently rector of St Mary Woolnoth, in the City of London. He has trained as a Psychosynthesis counsellor and supervisor, and works as a spiritual director and retreat giver. Since 2000 he has been the founder–director of the London Centre for Spirituality, based at St Edmund's Church in Lombard Street, which is developing as a resource for prayer, spiritual exploration and training for the City, the wider church and all living in the greater metropolitan area. The interface of psychology and spirituality, and the integration of faith and life, are two areas of particular interest to Andrew. His Masters dissertation was on the spiritual aspects of depression. Andrew has just completed a diploma in Charity Management at City University. His book *Journey into Joy*, a series of meditations on Easter, was published by SPCK in 2001.

**Rowan Douglas Williams** was born in Swansea in 1950. He was educated at Dynevor Secondary School, then at Christ's College, Cambridge, where he read Theology. After research in Oxford (on Christianity in Russia) he spent two years as a lecturer at Mirfield Theological College, near Leeds. From 1977 he spent nine years in academic and parochial work in Cambridge. From 1986 to 1992, Dr Williams was Professor of Theology at Oxford. He was enthroned as Bishop of

Monmouth in 1992, as Archbishop of Wales in 2000 and as the 104th Archbishop of Canterbury in 2003. Dr Williams has written a number of books on the history of theology and spirituality, and published collections of articles and sermons – as well as two books of poetry. He has been involved in various commissions on theology and theological education. He was a member of the Church Schools Review Group led by Lord Dearing and chaired the group that produced the report *Wales: a Moral Society?*. Dr Williams is a Fellow of the British Academy. His interests include music, fiction and languages. Since 1981 he has been married to Jane Paul, a lecturer in theology. They have a son and a daughter.

# Foreword

We seem to live in an age that may have given up faith in God, yet seems hooked on spirituality. It is also an age of urbanization, so a collection of essays that combines these interests is likely to scratch where we itch.

Before we sink into glib generalizations, however, let us also alert ourselves to the dangers for Christians in thinking that it is our task to assuage the cultural anxieties of our day. There is a danger that, in the face of indifference towards the institutional nature of the Christian Church, we might seek to offer a new, more popular and accessible brand, labelled 'Spirituality'.

The essays in this book alert us to some of the dangers that hover around such a viewpoint. They range from the personal to the theological, from experiences gathered on the 'mean streets' of the inner city to reflections on the politics of town planning in the era of postmodernism. They discuss the depiction of cities in Christian writing and in hymns, and recall how various groups have sought to explore the presence of God in sometimes very difficult urban settings. They direct our attention to the serious discipline of the theological discourse and show how it can engage with every aspect of life in the multifaceted society of urban Britain.

Above all, and despite the image of cities as places of pollution, chaos, squalor and deprivation, these essays are a celebration of the city as a place where both faith and human generosity can, and do, flourish. Running throughout is a theme of inclusivity and integration. Our attention is drawn to what is universally human, to forms of worship that shape a common language for devotion in personal and collective spheres, and to the ways in which urban life determines our Christian experience of God. How does this fit into the framework of

Christian mission, in its parochial and increasingly diverse expressions, and into the discipline of theological enquiry?

Andrew Walker is developing The London Centre for Spirituality, based at St Edmund the King, Lombard Street, as a city resource for prayer, training, exploration and development. In addition, the Centre fosters the skills of being and using a spiritual director or companion in ways that are as creative for the Christian as going to the gym and having a personal trainer are for city workers seeking a physically healthy lifestyle.

In some of the helpful discussion that has followed the recent suggestions of alternative ways of being Church today, the importance of values has been stated as central to our mission. Holiness is not merely the means to a missionary end: it is the transforming core value of our vocation to union with Jesus Christ. From holiness, a radical spirituality that sees humanity redeemed, beautiful, free and fully alive, comes social action in the Church and a relationship with those beyond it.

This new spirituality is constantly in search of ways to articulate its meaning, drawing the continuity of language, image and experience into fresh expression of eternal truth. A vital aspect of this endeavour is the inclusion of all human persons. You no longer have to be white, male, university-educated, married and Church of England.

The expression of the meaning of the civilization of love as expressive of the presence of God must, equally, transfuse our theological thought and discourse with that experience of prayer and interior knowledge that, like our words, confronts us with inadequacy, meaninglessness and dark not-knowing – prompting Michel de Certeau to write of the stubborn silence of God. It is on just such a majestic, awe-inspiring blank canvas that we dare to write of the 'things into which angels long to look' (1 Peter 1.12), the temerity of our reason, befriended by Scripture and the tradition, being humbled by the silent, tentative, prayerful experience of our spirits.

## Foreword

The presence and work of the London Centre for Spirituality points us to a quality of being human that embraces every condition in which we live, and every way of speaking, writing, painting, acting, singing, thinking, sculpting, dancing, working, praying, loving, eating and being with God. To speak of this as a civilization of love is to turn our attention to the human city, and our vocation to shape within it an image of the heavenly city of perfect unity and rest.

For London and all the citizens of our society, I hope that these essays will provide a statement of the dignity of the human spirit and an opportunity for hope, while facilitating a propensity for the knowledge of God and a reflection on the nature of the urban environment in which all these might flourish.

*Richard Chartres*
*Bishop of London*

# Preface

The idea for this collection of essays came to me in the run-up to the service at St Paul's Cathedral to mark the launch of the London Centre for Spirituality in September 2003. The Centre is based in the City of London, but serves as well the wider metropolitan area, both ecumenically and north and south of the river. The publication of the book marks the final phase of building at the Church of St Edmund the King in Lombard Street, providing a spirituality bookshop and better facilities for the disabled, in addition to the existing meeting rooms, hall and spirituality library.

The role of editor has not fallen to me before and I am grateful to Alison Barr at SPCK for her guidance, to the Centre staff for their patience and support and, above all, to Clare Thomson for her invaluable work and skill as our copy-editor. I hope this collection will prove a useful contribution, helping to draw out the rich potential of urban living and of the burgeoning interest in spirituality.

*Andrew Walker*
*Editor and Director,*
*The London Centre for Spirituality*

# 1

## Reclaiming faith

### Mark Oakley

———◆•◆———

### Introduction

Gerald Priestland once commented that 'as a naturally laid-back denomination the Church of England has always sought its thrills by frightening itself to death'. To put it another way, perhaps: 'An issue! An issue! We all fall down.' As a priest in this Church, I am only too aware at the moment that, as an institution, we have a remarkable tendency to focus on the peripheral, the political and the bureaucratic. If Evelyn Underhill was right when she said that the Church of England was a 'respectable suburb of the City of God', then we do transparently and frequently slip into the habits of bored, curtain-twitching housewives.

We are not the only people with this desire to be distracted. Not too long ago, it was reported that a boat in the USA was travelling up a river with its passengers celebrating a birthday party. All of a sudden, one of the revellers noticed that the boat was passing a nudist beach. Instantly, all the passengers ran to the right side of the boat to get a good look. Inevitably, the boat capsized and all the passengers got drenched in the water. This enacted parable of our time is revealing of the way that Christian communities can behave, craving titillation and a good gawp at others, and unaware of themselves and how such behaviour flies in the face of all that the gospel of Jesus Christ teaches about human relations. Perhaps, rather than laugh at the ironies here, we should develop our ability for what the seventeenth-century Anglican Divines called 'the gift of tears'.

If this were the only story I could tell as a priest, however, it would be a sorry state of affairs and cause for resignation. It is not, though. As a priest who has worked in Central London, I have another, much happier, story to relate about Christian faith in human lives, the attempt to celebrate the eternal God in our midst. It is a story about commitment to this pursuit and the translation of the Christian hope into a non-negotiable care of the marginalized. The Church I read about in the newspapers often seems very remote from the churches I encounter in my locality. The issues that seem to make head-lines are not the issues that clergy and congregations spend their energies on. Thank God for that.

Those thousands who walk into our churches, for whatever reason, can still feel both uncomfortable (this is a place unlike the high street) and somehow at home (this is a place where the human soul can catch its breath). This initial sense of both strangeness and familiarity that our buildings, and our congregations, can give voice to is at the heart of who we are, as a Church, in this created world. What I hope to do in this short essay is to look at these intimations of the sacred – the rumours of God – and to see how the faith that often builds itself up on them is shaped by their being listened to in a twenty-first-century city.

## Coming to the city

By birth and upbringing I am a Shropshire lad. Shropshire is a beautiful county and a well-kept secret. In the north it levels into the Cheshire plain with its own lake district; in the west it is protected by shadowed border hills and upland heath; and in the south it melts into the soft contours of Herefordshire. It is a place of natural magnificence and proud histories, not least of farming, the Industrial Revolution and the county's many market towns, which, in the words of Thomas Hardy, are 'the pole, focus and nerve knot of the surrounding country life'. It is also a county without a city.

Coming to London to study at university was, therefore, quite a shock. I don't need to rehearse the ingredients that make living in a large city so distinct from life elsewhere, but I was bowled over by the sheer colour and confusion: the choices, the galleries, theatres and concerts; the streets' noise, yet their anonymity; the displays of wealth; the 'push and shove-ness' of everything; and the remarkable diversity. When I travelled to church in Bethnal Green or walked up the Strand at night, I was shocked by the poverty and homelessness too. It didn't take that long for this new environment, added to the new theological thoughts I was having with my excellent teachers, to push me back to Shropshire for a couple of weeks to re-cover from stress-related shingles.

Nearly 20 years later, ordained and Rector of St Paul's, in the heart of Covent Garden, I was still cautious of much that the city encourages and promotes, not least the collective hypnosis of what makes for being cool, fashionable and acceptable. Spiritually, I was aware of the truth that Graham Ward identifies when commenting on the Bible's ambivalence towards cities, the first being built by the murderer Cain: 'The origins of the city, for the Bible, seem to lie in masculine ex-pressions of defiance, insecurity, the need to find substitutions and consolations for the loss of God, and the desire perhaps to take the place of that God, to become a dynasty.' As well as the hopes and dreams of city-builders, there is a dark sense of judgment by God, writes Ward, on 'all the lofty towers and all the sheer walls' (Isaiah 2.12), filtered through alternative visions of the heavenly and divinely manufactured City.[1]

These health warnings necessarily placed on city life, how-ever, did not stop me from enjoying life and work in one of the biggest cities of all. The social atomism that threatens the ability to collaborate, the opting out from reality in favour of a virtual one, the signs that our cities are turning into 'radically eclectic places where each pursues his or her own consumer interests under the ever-watchful eye of surveillance cameras ready to pinpoint when radical difference flares up into riot'[2] are, naturally, deep concerns for a city's social life and desire for the common good. The challenges, however, must not paralyse us into a cynicism about the present or future. Cynicism is a grave-digging exercise. It cannot, by its very nature, be constructive.

The vitality, surprises, pulse and opportunities of so much that makes up a day there (encountering people from every possible background, nation, world-view and income bracket, with experiences of the full measure of human suffering, hurt, privilege and joy) overwhelmingly inspirits, as well as exhausts, one. If Gandhi was right in saying that before we try to meet God anywhere else, we should try to meet him in the next person we meet, then the city is full of spiritual potential. When Italo Calvino, however, perceived that 'each city receives its form from the desert it opposes',[3] he alerted us to our fears and our desires – and that is always a good place to start on the spiritual quest.

## Intimations

It has been said for a number of years now, by such sociologists as Grace Davie, for example,[4] that, contrary to much of what one reads by opinion columnists, there is not actually a wholesale shift in the Western world towards a secular society where religious faith is no more. Rather, there is suspicion of institutions and what one might call 'institutional truth' – compromised, shaped by the logic of expediency and moulded on Caiaphas – and there is an erosion of interest in ritual participation and regular commitment within a particular faith community. Steve Bruce is surely on to something when he notes that 'individualism threatened the communal basis of religious belief and behaviour, while rationality removed many of the purposes of religion and rendered many of its beliefs implausible'.[5] There is, however, a considerable persistence of genuine intrigue in the possibilities of God and the sense of the numinous, with the idea of reality being trustworthy, with ethics and the intuition that life is a gift and is not finalized at death, and so on. It is as if people don't quite believe their unbelief.

This is particularly evident in the very centre of our cities, where our churches are used as places sporadically visited for reflection, the lighting of a candle, de-stressing or listening to a concert, but not so much for regular communal involvement. They are drop-in centres for those with a homeless, often unfocused, faith. Much of a church's work in the city centre is to make the visitor comfortable, to enable him or her to pray if possible, to tease out the resonances of the Christian tradition in as many ways as possible, so that the deepest longing of all, that for God's freshness, is attended to with dignity and the desire to uphold the individual's integrity. Meister Eckhart believed that 'God is like a person who clears his throat while hiding and so gives himself away.' The challenge to the churches at the moment is to unveil whether there might be a divine presence in so much contemporary darkness, and to encourage the energy that is still there in people's lives to listen out for the divine coughs and tickles. So much of my time is spent with people hovering on the boundaries of the church, often unsure as to whether the Church has integrity, and whether their own might be maintained if they played some part in it, however minor. Is there an understanding of Christian faith that is plausible but also a challenge, wise but fresh? Is there a Christianity available in which I can remain honest and en route? I believe very much that this is time well spent if the Church is to remain more than a club or special-interest society.

The opportunities for conversation on such topics at the moment are endless, and it is essential that Christian people, in their search for a contemporary apologetic, do not become apologetic. We can, and should, express our hatred for all that the Church has done in the past and in the present to focus on, and even utilize, human depravity rather than dignity, and to injure and kill people as well as faith. Yet when we call ourselves back to the very essentials of what the Church is for – the worship of God, the care of God's people – we cannot afford to be anything less than confident for, and in, the gospel and faith in God.

## Faith in the city?

When the West End got too much, I sometimes took myself off to Primrose Hill for some quiet, and for a marvellous view of the city. If it's a windy day, there are usually plenty of children flying kites. A kite is a good focus for faith: the spiritual adventure, bouncing about, ducking and diving, on the winds of the spirit and the currents of the day. It is full of colour, a sort of moving meeting point between earth and heaven, at times so strong it is difficult to control, yet also sometimes plummeting, tired, unable to dance. A kite is also tied to a string, and faith is grounded, as well as free-flying; it has, as it were, roots. The thread of faith has to be knotted, or else the currents of novelty and mere opinion can carry it off and it is never seen again. When the poet Gerard Manley Hopkins prayed to the Lord of Life to 'send our roots rain', he knew that if we lose our memory, our threads to our inheritance, we lose our identity, both as individuals and as a Church.

Because of the way we use the word today, however, many people probably think that faith is the same as belief, that it is synonymous with holding certain intellectual propositions to be true. When faith was given the definite article and became 'the faith', it reinforced this intuition. To believe in God today means that you are expressing your conviction that a spiritual reality called God exists. But it is very likely that our ancestors did not mean this when they said they believed in God. As the *Oxford English Dictionary* states, belief was the earlier word for what is now commonly called faith: that is, putting one's trust in God, giving your heart to, rather than having an opinion about. Medieval Christians, for instance, might have thought that the Devil existed, but they would never have dreamt of saying that they believed in the Devil. On the contrary, he was to be renounced. Instead, I believe in God, they said: that is, I entrust myself to him, with all my fragility, mess and questions.

In an environment in which one is used to talking about religion as fundamentalist and intolerant in character, belief today has come to mean having certain unshakeable intellectual convictions about *x* and *y*. And faith in God has come to be seen as something very similar. People therefore think that the opposite of faith must be doubt; after all, part of belief cannot be not believing. The effect this has on people's lives is well known to us. It also means that a vast majority of people think that other people are making a better job of being a Christian, or whatever, than they are because they are aware only of their confusions and reticence. People will say that they can't go to church because they don't believe enough. They can't tick all the credal boxes. They feel on the margins, and religion feels more like a circle that is drawn to keep them out rather than include them.

Those who are seeking faith in the city first need to work out what they are looking for and expecting. Cities today can encourage impatience – certainly a danger to faith, as to any relationship. We might expect too much, too soon from faith, which is, after all, a journey, not an arrival. I would hope, then, that we might reclaim an understanding of faith that flies free from belief in the modern sense, in order to nestle next to belief in its former meaning: the business of trying to trust and live with God over time, and in flickering communion with him. Might we be ready to be a bit controversial, in the spirit of the French thinker Jacques Ellul,[6] when he confronts us with the reflection that belief provides answers to people's questions, while faith never does? That is, people believe in order to find assurance, a solution, a system of ideas. Faith, especially biblical faith, is completely different. The purpose of revelation is not to supply us with explanations or propositions, but to get us to listen to questions, radical addresses to ourselves and the world we are making. Belief talks and wallows in words, takes the initiative; faith waits, remains on guard, picks up signs, seeks to discern complex parables, listens to a silence poised for God. Belief looks for regimentation. Faith can be lonely: it knows that holiness means being separated somehow. Belief is reassuring, makes you feel safe. Faith is forever placing you on the razor's edge. Belief can order God and normalize. Faith knows this can't be done and, as it were, puts the odd back into God. Belief relates to ideas. Faith knows that ideas can get in the way; it embraces paradox and silence, and often lives with city-like confusion. If I discern the stirrings of faith in me, the first rule is not to deceive myself, not to abandon myself to beliefs indiscriminately. I have to subject them to rigorous criticism. I have to listen to denials and attacks on them. Faith will not stand for half-truths.

Faith is not the business of signing up to intellectual propositions. It is, rather, the business of trying to live and move and have our being in God, source of life and love, and as a Christian, to engage with God as I encounter him in Jesus Christ. Perhaps the opposite of faith is not doubt but certainty? People don't tend to take a 'leap of belief', after all. This is not to say that the attempt to define Christian beliefs, priorities and hopes should not be made. On the contrary, we need imaginative and generous creativity to continue its work here. Yet faith and trust in God, in the spirit of Jesus Christ, is primary to these musings, and may even have to challenge them when hardened into something lifeless and thoughtlessly ritualized – again, in the spirit of Jesus Christ.

I once heard someone who was talking about Australian sheep farming say that it differs from other sorts because the sheep aren't fenced in; they simply gather together around the watering hole. Is that the difference between belief and faith? Is this an important distinction that we need confidently to make as we engage with those who wonder whether they can ever find a place in a community of faith?

## *The Divine method*

Evelyn Underhill once referred to the 'Divine method of hiddenness and humility'. Her study of the Christian mystics had led her to conclude that God could not be grasped by reason or intellect, and that 'dimness and lostness of the mind' is a necessary part of the journey into God.[7] She also saw that God is more likely to be encountered in an act of compassion, or a dethronement of the self, than in a ritual or doctrinal purity code. God's hiddenness invites us to learn the lessons of humility – including that of it being the case that God is to be shared before he is understood. In the theatre, the lights need to be dimmed if there is to be a scene change. Our spiritual life follows a similar pattern. Yann Martel's novel *The Life of Pi*[8] reminds us of the story of Lord Krishna who, when he was a cowherd, invited all the milkmaids to dance with him. Each girl, in her great excitement, dances with the sweet Lord, who has made himself so abundant as to be in the arms of each and every girl. The moment the girls become possessive, however, the instant each girl believes that the Lord dances with her and nobody else, he vanishes. So it is, writes Martel, 'that we should not be jealous with God'. It is a case of Mystery teaching us manners (respect, love and modesty).

The Divine method defies so much of our present pre-occupation. Underhill, writing several decades ago, is as contemporary as ever when she writes of our lives: 'We mostly spend those lives conjugating three verbs: to Want, to Have and to Do. Craving, clutching, and fussing . . . forgetting that none of these verbs have any ultimate significance, except so far as they are transcended by . . . the fundamental verb, to Be."[9]

It seems to me that our cities are wonderful places for us to learn more about the Divine method of being alive. Our constant encounter with difference and our fight to be a citizen, rather than just a consumer, are both pregnant opportunities for spiritual growth. Like all holy potential, however, these things are also ripe for developments that are destructive and harmful if used in such a spirit. Difference can be a dangerous fuel on angry fires. Our dissatisfaction and restlessness as shoppers can also lead to some precarious places of escape. Likewise, the good intention to be a democratic citizen can become ugly and self-righteous – ending in that perfect democracy that cannot admit that its sovereign, the people, might occasionally be wrong. The Church can call itself truly catholic only when it takes its relentless capacity for friendships seriously and works in partnership to make sure our cities live rather than exist, through critical solidarity with its partners and faith in the Divine method of releasing community at the expense of ego.

## *Provisions for faith*

As those in our cities learn what faith might mean, and how it might be further explored with our churches as places of prayer and education, it is important to stress how a city can provide remarkable encouragement for those exploring truth and religious faith. For a start, there are all the theatres, where life and humanity are placed under the microscope and the picture is enlarged for our learning. If the theatre is thought to be just a branch of entertainment, it will, of course, be easy to dismiss. If, however, it is seen as a gymnasium for underused imaginations (as our churches should be too), then it is an ally to those who want to see the invisible, the undercurrents that rule our lives, and a diving board for delving beyond the surface. Religion and theatre are ancient cousins, and it is time for more family get-togethers. Churches in the cities should be trying to use their space to encourage all the arts in their celebration and exploration of creative and non-verbal truth and beauty. Poets, actors, dancers and musicians should be supported wherever possible, and come to see the church as a place where their work is taken seriously in a common pursuit for the real. It is not a rare experience for artists and people of faith to discover in each other's worlds echo chambers of those truths that matter deeply to them. When St Augustine wondered as to membership of the Church, he pondered: 'Many seem to be within who are in reality without, and others seem to be without who are in reality within.'[10]

Similarly, the cities offer many opportunities for service to those who need assistance and human support. The various volunteer bodies and charities, along with the other excellent work that goes on day by day to fight alienation and poverty, are the places where Christ is still met and reverenced. The story of the monk who set off on a pilgrimage for Jerusalem is spiritually wise. He prepared for many years, studied the maps and said the right prayers. He longed to be one of the pilgrims who journey three times around the city's sacred walls. Eventually, he was given permission and set off. Just down the road, he came across a hungry man who was begging for his children. The monk gave him his money, then, to the alarm of the man, walked around the poor man three times, listened to him and chatted with him, restating the man's sense of worth. The monk then bade the man farewell and returned straight away to his brethren. They were astonished that he was back so soon. Hadn't he gone to visit Jerusalem? 'No', replied the monk. 'Jerusalem visited me.' In our longings for sacred places to rest and be at peace, we can often miss the way God comes to us. There are few excuses in the city.

There is an important postscript to all this. As Diarmaid MacCulloch[11] points out in his tremendous recent book on the Reformation, in a small country church in Buckinghamshire there lurks an interesting addition to the church architecture. Holding up the arch at the entrance to the chancel, the most sacred part of the building, are two fourteenth-century carved stone figures. One of them is of a man crouched on all fours, displaying his ample buttocks towards the high altar where, day by day, the priest of the parish presided at the Mass. It is uncertain why such a cheeky sculpture was placed there. Was it a warning to a lazy priest? Did it express the laity's impatience when the clergy did not perform their tasks properly? Was it a symbol of Satan, out to distract the church from its true work? Whatever the reason, I wonder whether we could do with a little revival of such imagery? For whatever other things that medieval sculptor did, he reminded the priest and the people of the church not to get above themselves or take themselves too seriously.

There is a frightening mood of puritanism around in the contemporary Church, and I am convinced this mood shadows our evangelism and our building-up of trust outside the church community. ('Let them take heed', wrote Francis Bacon, referring to the Puritans of his own day, 'that it be not true which one of their adversaries said, that they have but two small wants, knowledge and love.') To be serious about our work does not mean being humourless. In fact, as we know in other fields, those who cannot laugh are those who live with the deeper insecurities.

The medieval church practices that occurred in places such as Bavaria have much to teach us still. When, for instance, they celebrated Christ's harrowing of hell, what MacCulloch calls his 'cosmic hooliganism', the Christians at Hof made a solemn procession with a crucifix out of the church, but found its way barred by a crowd of local youths dressed as devils. After a lot of argy-bargy, with tremendous noise and slamming of doors, the devils fled the scene, throwing down their flaming torches. There is something wonderfully elemental about this sort of sacred theatre. Similarly, the lowering of a carved wooden dove through a church roof in Eichstäd on the feast of Pentecost must have been a charming sight. The bucketfuls of water that came down with it, however, reminding the churchgoers that the Holy Spirit was not wooden and controlled, but the One who drenches you with a cold shock, must have been startling. The member of the congregation most thoroughly soaked became the town's 'Whitsunbird' for the coming year. Religion that includes shouts of laughter, as well as roars of rage, is not that common today, and it is time for some resuscitation. If our city churches cannot find room for this holy tomfoolery, what can?

The levelling of irony, the release of uncomfortable perception and the enjoyment of each other are all vital if religious faith is not to turn sour. Like the Holy Spirit, humour both comforts us and disturbs us. Those of us who try to live lives of Christian faith in a city environment are only too aware of the absurdities of much that we end up doing and saying. We also know that in such a busy and atomized environment, finding the space to laugh with others is no small thing. No wonder the Koran teaches that: 'He who makes his companions laugh, deserves paradise.'

## Conclusion

It is no secret that the Church is not as strong, influential or as popular as it once was. I reckon that those of us who still find our faith nurtured by much of the Church's worship, and her invitation to Christian discipleship and commitment, must have a Wordsworthian attitude: 'We will grieve not, rather find/ Strength in what remains behind' (from *Intimations of Immortality*). There are certainly signs that, even though many commentators suggest that only the secular can be tolerant (plainly absurd) and that faith leads people into irrational thinking and inhumane acts (sometimes true), many people still believe that the rumours of God may be correct and worthy of proper attention by the living of a humane life. John Gray has recently asked whether the repression of the religious impulse explains the excessive rigidity of much secular thought.[12]

Whatever, much of pure atheistic thinking's fundamentalist character is still deficient to many others who are, as yet, uncommitted to a faith community. It is also true that these people know deep down that, on the other side as it were, bumper-sticker theology and quick-fix certainties are inauthentic too. 'True theology is a species of poetry that, read quickly or encountered in a hubbub of noise, makes no sense.'[13] People who are looking for something do not travel very fast. They travel patiently, with all senses alive. We therefore need schools of prayer, spiritual learning and places where the riches of our Christian heritage are opened up in accessible and non-defensive ways. We need places to reveal the uncomfortable simplicity of Jesus Christ and the questions asked of us in the Scriptures. We need places that will teach us the vitalities of rhythm and discipline in the spiritual life. We need more of what Bacon's Puritans lacked: knowledge and love. I, among many, then, am delighted that London now has such a new Centre for Spirituality.

The heartbeat of faith is desire. When we think we somehow possess God, we stop desiring him; faith becomes cold, and can look to replace itself with the comforts of a propositional belief where God becomes an object of discussion rather than the Subject to whom we relate. The Divine method of God giving us just enough to look for him but never enough to fully find him – a God who keeps us on pilgrimage towards the heavenly city yet who offers glimpses of who he is in the creative, and in compassion and mercy – is, to my mind, our deepest encouragement to keep faith in the city.

# 2

# Urbanization, the Christian Church and the human project

Rowan Williams

━━━◆◆◆━━━

It's said fairly often that the biblical narrative begins in a garden and ends in a city. Something about the way God leads us through history is linked, it seems, with our growth towards a situation in which we take a more and more creative role in shaping our environment – not just in cultivating the natural environment in which God has placed us, like Adam, but in building a complex kind of home that is shared by others, with whom we have to negotiate, whose concerns we have to ponder and interact with. The garden is a good image for some aspects of our growth with God. It may seem the most obvious image (*The Garden of the Soul* was, after all, the title of the most influential English book of Catholic piety in the modern era[1]). But it is the *City* of God that dominates the most sophisticated reflection on the nature of God's community.

And here we are likely to feel a bit of dissonance. Cities these days are not the soberly elegant city states of medieval Italy, or even the burgeoning, buzzing, self-confident (and hideously polluted) industrial and commercial centres of the nineteenth and early twentieth centuries in Europe and the USA. 'Urbanization' is now one of the words that most vividly describes the demographic crisis and human tragedy of late modernity. It goes with globalization: it signifies the inexorable drift towards structures and landscapes – including landscapes of economic relations and social possibilities – that are in various ways inhuman. These are structures and landscapes that proclaim the powerlessness of individuals and of small-scale societies to exercise any creative role in moulding the environment. They speak of spaces that are not mapped or shaped with human beings in mind – uncharted and undifferentiated space where nobody feels at home, environments that carry a message about the insignificance of the aspirations and preferences of persons and small groups. If this is the face of the contemporary city, how can it be a place where the spirit can flourish? I know that the current city landscape is often a scene of new energy and vitality; but I make no apology for concentrating in these reflections on the cost of urbanization, the background of helplessness that shadows the most vibrant of city cultures and seems not to grow any less disturbing, whatever the 'upper' and sometimes more visible sectors of urban society are doing.

It is hard to imagine the urbanizing process going backwards. At the very least, we can't now imagine a situation where communities stop being mobile and mixed. We have become used to cities as places of variety – places where those with purchasing power can exercise the maximal amount of consumer freedom; but also places where difference between groups need not always break down into savage hostility, because there is room for some space between communities. It is true that this collapses pretty often, and that new tribal loyalties are created, and so new conflicts: one of the marks of modern urban living is the 'gated' community, areas of prosperity surrounded by state-of-the-art security. But there is something about the space of urban attention that makes it attractive (and always has made it attractive) for the minority. Your life is less likely to be seen as a threat by a close-knit and quite homogeneous majority community. And precisely because minorities find a voice in urban life, they can begin to influence majorities: radical change comes from urban, rather than rural, life.

Urban life, then, is at once dangerous and creative; at once destructive of much that is humanly significant and a seedbed in which change can germinate and people become able to think of new possibilities. If we are trying to be clear about how to pray and how to be a disciple in the modern city, we have to avoid equally a sentimental view of urban life, one that celebrates its entrepreneurial energy and range of choices, and an apocalyptic picture that laments its unrelieved inhumanity. We have to ask what the significant available choices are, and how they serve the uncovering of God's image.

So, what follows is at best a rough sketch of the sort of themes and concerns that might inform an 'urban spirituality' today. It is not a programme or a prescription: one of the lessons that has to be learnt is that it won't do to impose an agenda from outside. Urban populations need to understand for themselves where and who they are, and what their possibilities might be. And the role of the Church needs some careful thinking through. Sam Wells, in a particularly insightful essay on the role of the Church in community regeneration,[2] has noted the problem that can arise if the Church is seen as one interest group among others, bidding competitively for scarce resources or seeking to control the self-definition of communities. The contribution of the Church must always be something on another level from that of the various bodies struggling for dominance and access. It must simply offer a radically different imaginative landscape, in which people can discover possibilities of change – and perhaps of 'conversion' in the most important sense, a 'turning around' of values and priorities that grows from trust in God.

Wells suggests ways in which the distinctive practices of the Church – baptism, communion, Bible-reading and prayer – both signal and make possible alternative accounts of what life might be. Building on what he says, I want to suggest a few possible priorities for those concerned with the life of the spirit in the modern city.

17

The first has to do with the use and organization of *time*. As we have noted, one of the characteristics of the modern urban environment is the growing homogenization of *space*: people live in settings that are more 'flattened' and undifferentiated than the village and the small town. Mass housing, the modern insistence on 'zoning' in urban planning (so that residential and retail properties aren't found side by side) and the general gulf between the processes of planning and the decisions of actual inhabitants mean that a lot of (especially newer) urban landscapes are interchangeable. The prevailing patterns of retail commerce reinforce this: the same retail chains are found everywhere, with identical merchandise. So one of the first questions about the spirit and the city must be what can be recovered of a more differentiated atmosphere; what in the environment can speak of difference, of individualities that are not just exchangeable the world over, and so of real exchange between diverse persons and communities.

For the Christian, this matters because of our belief that the optimal form of Christian community, the Body of Christ, is one in which diversity of gifts and the movement of giving and receiving are all-important. If people are to be brought a little closer to this optimal community style, there must be ways of affirming and celebrating difference. Religious communities are all agreed that time needs breaking up, punctuating, by festival (and fasting too) – by rhythms that mark and shape the passage of time and recognize different emotions, different stages in growth, recognizing that dimension of human living that involves process and the shifts of 'climate' in the life of mind and heart. Breaking up time into weeks and months and years is only the tip of the iceberg; all societies until the modern age have structured the weeks and the years in more elaborate ways, usually coinciding with the agricultural year. A society that has moved away from these rhythms either becomes obsessed with using time 'profitably' – or it sets out to rediscover rhythms of celebration that can survive the urban environment, the relative distance from the change of the seasons that is inevitable in city life.

Andrew Shanks's splendid and provocative book *God and Modernity*[3] puts a case for 'calendar reform' – for a new civic consciousness that organizes time around freshly thought-out historical commemorations (the fall of the Berlin Wall, the legacy of the slave trade and its ending). This, he suggests, would give us a corporate sense both of a present time that had pauses and movements, like a musical composition, and a past time that had both triumphs and failures. But this in turn suggests – whatever may become of such proposals at the level of a whole nation – that an urban environment needs the same rhythm of movement and pause at local level. One of the things that anyone concerned with this should reflect on is what can be done to make public, and to celebrate reflectively, the things that a community regards as defining and important. Perhaps it's often a matter of hanging some of this onto existing festival dates in the Church's calendar – commemorating specific local trauma in Holy Week, using Mothering Sunday to say something about the joys and challenges of parenting in a community, perhaps to remember the local difficulties or tragedies of children, certainly to make a point about communication between generations. It is certainly not about replacing the Church's calendar with something completely other. It is both seeking new and independent commemorations and, where appropriate, including local and particular history within the Church's story – while being careful not to swallow it, exploit it or make it no more than an illustration of some pre-existing Christian moral. A hard task, but not impossible. And the ethnic and religious variety of the modern urban scene means that the available religious calendars are not going to be exclusively Christian: nothing to regret there, as many pastors and workers in the urban context would testify.

The weekend may be a lost cause in many communities, thanks to that triumph of functional and acquisitive philosophy that was the legitimizing of Sunday trading. But this does not mean that we can or should give up on the question of how to structure the time in which people live; and the weekly rhythm is not the only one possible, however much we might feel nostalgic for it. Urban society's time needs punctuations if it is not to become a view without landmarks. There are matters to celebrate and mourn together, if we can listen and find out; and, as we do, it may become possible to find ways of marking times and seasons that are not artificial.

A second possibility. The urban landscape is characteristically characterless. What, then, gives 'character'? I have a recollection of a woman in a South Welsh urban setting who had decided (she lived alone and could determine her domestic timetable) to set aside her small living room as a place where other women in the neighbourhood could come for silence at almost any time in the week. If they turned up, they could sit alone or they could be quietly accompanied. In a landscape without *spatial* 'pauses', gaps for reflection, holy places, she had simply decided to create something of this sort, in a prosaic and accessible way. So the question is, who in a community might have the resource (physical and spiritual) to provide space of this kind? There are often those who are recognizable as having made space in themselves, who, in a pressurized and crowded human environment, bring a sense of giving others room to breathe. How can they be helped and supported to keep open the offer their lives imply? And can their gifts be linked with actual places, like my friend's living room? This is a different question from one that is often raised in this context: the question (equally important) of how you learn to recognize the places that, as a matter of fact, are regarded as significant public space in a community, even as holy, charged with meaning or memory. But it is a question worth addressing. And somewhere between the provision of space for quiet in households and the recognition of publicly accessible significant space is a phenomenon that seems to have become more prominent in recent years – an interest, mostly among voluntary groups, in reclaiming small public spaces as memorial gardens, protected places for quiet. The vastly impressive Soul in the City summer campaigns, which involve young people of Christian conviction descending in great numbers on an urban environment in need of help and reclamation, quite often find themselves involved in projects of this sort. And their work is a regular reminder of the more general point that the message that an environment is in some sense simply *manageable* – that it does not have to spiral out of control as far as basic cleanliness and usability are concerned – is a serious element of what the good news can entail in a physically degraded setting.

A third area is perhaps more obvious. Urban life is lived under the sign of anonymous exchange; should not any community concerned with spiritual health therefore be on the watch for those forms of exchange that avoid the anonymous? This is not to suggest that the Church become an enthusiastic sponsor of the black market that is the main form of economic activity in a good many areas of acute urban deprivation! Black markets are really just another kind of unaccountable and exploitative power mechanism. But local trading schemes, micro-credit initiatives and so on are structures with well-defined and close local accountability, a good record in developing skills and restoring a sense of limited, but real, control over economic circumstances, and a low level of capital and organizational outlay. They generate self-respect and broad and forward-looking vision for oneself and others. They are something that a local faith community can contribute to very effectively, offering a ready-made pool of volunteers. More importantly, though, they represent a challenge to the assumption of urban modernity that serious power and effective organization has always to be centralized. And as I have suggested, there are good theological reasons for resisting this assumption, to the degree that it takes for granted a pattern of social relation that has little room for mutuality.

I mention in passing here the Habitat for Humanity schemes of house-building that have been so successful in many American urban settings, but have still to be taken fully seriously in the UK. Here, as with local micro-credit, the point is to give a degree of choice and control to local groups that is *not* simply a form of generalized consumer choice. In a context where a majority in the community have limited economic freedom, what is needed is not a range of options offered by a mass provider, but a few realistic paths for action that will affirm that it is possible, after all, to have a creative impact on your environment.

All I have said so far is based on the assumption that the search for spiritual seriousness in the modern and postmodern urban setting takes place against a material background designed with minimal attention to the needs of concrete human community. The strategies outlined inevitably have an air of damage limitation. And in any comprehensive look at the spirit in the city, we need also to think about a possible future in which it would not always be necessary to take for granted that the physical environment would be inimical to ordinary human flourishing. The challenge is how to get theology onto the agenda of planning, locally and nationally (though without necessarily letting on that it is theology). We live in an age of paradox. We have, as a culture, become very interested in 'sick buildings', in the mistakes made in the recent past about where and how natural light is allowed in, in Feng Shui and all that goes with it, in the inadequacy of Le Corbusier's infamous definition of a house as 'a machine for living in'; yet we persist in habits of large-scale planning (and, indeed, in the construction of public buildings) that suggest we are really gnostics who believe in a total separation of body and spirit. We ought to have learnt that the spirit's welfare is not a subject we can sensibly discuss without both a science and a wisdom of the environment. We have to take seriously what physical and psychological research tells us about the effects of certain material structures on how we think and feel about ourselves; and we need to have a positive vision of humanity and of what a freely co-operative humanity might require – a vision shaped not just by guesswork and vague goodwill, but by that fundamental Christian conviction about the Body of Christ as the best form of human togetherness.

To talk about 'urban spirituality' must be to talk about the politics of the built environment as well as what particular persons can do within a given urban setting. There are, as we have seen, several ways in which an environment can be humanized in such a way as to bring out the possibilities of a humanity more attuned to God and to its own depths. But those who have a continuing concern for the health of the spirit will have to probe further, to ask some questions about how and where decisions are made, and how a difference can be made to those processes. The cluster of skills and tactics summed up in the philosophy of 'community organizing' will not of themselves deliver spiritual depth, but without some such pointers as to how access to levers of power in respect of the built environment is to be secured, lives will continue to be threatened by fragmentation, because the material setting is a daily reminder of powerlessness. And in any and every programme for regeneration, Christian believers should be actively asking about the human scale of anything proposed for the material environment as a necessary aspect of caring for the spiritual welfare of the people involved. It ought not to be so unusual as it seems to be for these matters to be raised; but an approach to community regeneration that looks only for economic growth, improved choice, better access to development funds and so on will fail in enlarging the spiritual horizons of people if it is cut off from these awkward issues around the messages that an environment conveys.

In this as in so many areas, the education of the spirit is inseparably bound to highly practical challenges. If – as St Francis de Sales is supposed to have said – spiritual direction begins when people are helped to walk more slowly, talk more slowly and eat more slowly, then the life of the spirit in the city will entail asking about the size of rooms in public buildings, the flow of traffic in streets, the levels of atmospheric pollution, the maintenance of parks, galleries and libraries, the space available for children in public – and countless other matters where decisions are regularly taken as though none of these could possibly be an issue. We have begun to notice the problems, and we are, thank God, unlikely to revert to the barbarous planning philosophies of the mid twentieth century. Yet we still treat separate zoning as unquestionable; we still design residential areas without visible points of focus, as if they were just an assembly of individual residences; we still struggle to get spiritual health onto the agenda of groups planning and discussing regeneration. We have some way to go.

Before ending this brief reflection on the challenges, I want to add a few words about the definition of spirituality itself. To summarize points that have been made in a good many places in recent years, we need to rescue 'spirituality' from some of the ways in which it has been domesticated, even trivialized, in recent years. A popular and a vague word, it demands – especially for the Christian – an anchorage in some specific convictions about human beings and their possibilities. Without this, it becomes only a code for techniques of making people feel a bit better about themselves; whereas the life of the spirit ought also to make people uncomfortable about themselves and their environment, critical and creative, open to things being different. If it is true, as I think it is, that 'spirit' in biblical Christianity is a word describing the human self in tune with the truth of its own nature and with God, it is always a term that involves thinking about human interrelation. When the New Testament speaks of the life of 'spirit', it speaks of the virtues and gifts of life together. It assumes that to grow in the spiritual life is to become free to give to others what has been given to you – hence the belief that the Christian community is where spirit is most freely at work, through the infusion of *God's* Spirit.

So the image of the City of God makes some sense. To the extent that urban life represents, in the history of human culture, a move beyond the sheer struggle for self-sufficiency, a move towards diversified community and a sharpened sense of the variety of goods (material, intellectual, imaginative) that people can exchange with each other, it is an appropriate metaphor for Christian community. Like all metaphors, it brings its own problems. Using the urban image might lead us to think, at some level, that the ideal community was one for which the natural cycle of the seasons or the contingency of the weather was insignificant, one in which actual locality didn't matter, where all situations were equal and interchangeable – and where persons were equal primarily in the sense of being interchangeable, where everything had a price. The image needs correctives: the City is also a Body; the Church is also a kinship group; the landscape of the new creation is also a restored garden.

Only if we keep this balance in mind, the inevitable mutual correction of images in our theology, can we use the metaphor of God's people as city to confront the menaces of urbanization as we experience it today. The city in the 'developed' world is not in a good state, its centre empty of homes, its properties insecure, its shopping malls dangerous territories for the disaffected and bored and violent to gather. The city in the 'developing' world is in far worse condition; it gathers the destitute and drives them further into destitution. Both aspects of the modern urban phenomenon speak of the gulf between ordinary human aspiration and the decisions that a global market seems to impose. Yet neither is simply a nightmare of predestined misery. The city in the Western world still generates unexpected co-operation and local communal energy; the city in Africa or Latin America has, in its town-ships or *favelas*, countless instances of people humanizing their setting, making a territory, however apparently featureless, their own. Within the harsh conditions of urban life for the major-ity of city-dwellers, there is a reality present that obstinately speaks of matters that are at odds with the 'flat landscape', the undifferentiated, delocalized atmosphere I have mentioned so often in these pages. Those whose responsibility it is to discern where the spirit (and the Spirit) are at work will need to be alert to these half-hidden examples of internal protest, internal dissociation from the dehumanizing assumptions that appear to prevail. What I have touched on earlier in this paper is simply a handful of ways in which the Church might contri-bute here – and might open a way to the story of that city whose founder is God, and to citizenship in that community. The gospel can be preached and heard anywhere, in any social or economic conditions. True, but this is never an alibi for failing to ask how we help it to be heard, and how we work to create persons and communities for whom the hearing of the good news will be less encumbered by the various slaveries that may delay or distort response to the joy and the challenge. Evangelizing entails a share in the work of humanizing the city. Jesus looked at Jerusalem and wept; he entered the city and suffered; he instructed his friends to wait there for the coming of power from on high, for the promise of the Father. Those who now try to be his disciples often have a fair amount of weeping to do over the city; they may find themselves shar-ing in some measure his exile and rejection from the circles where decisions are made (and so sharing what the deprived and disadvantaged in the modern city know). But most im-portantly, they are to wait in the city, having heard the news of his new life, looking out for the promise of the Father, ready to explore their own 'citizenship of heaven' and to open it up to others in such a way as to transform the citizenship and the cities of this earth.

# 3

## *Hymns and the city*

### Rosalind Brown

———◆◆◆———

Hymns are essentially a combination of text and tune that we use to express ourselves, together, to God. A good hymn is both personal and corporate: it uses words and music that I can sing together with others and with integrity, yet it also expresses my own thoughts and desires. A hymn that is too specific may not be usable by a group, because the group does not identify with it; a hymn that is too general may gloss over my situation and leave me voiceless. The best hymns are written out of specific experience, but move beyond the catalytic situation to express universal truth, to become words and music that together we want to own and sing to God, that take on a life of their own every time they are sung, because each congregation embodies the hymn differently. A hymn can 'sing' very differently in different contexts, a fact that is of significance when we consider hymns and the city, since a hymn about the city sung in a deeply rural area may offer a different spiritual experience from the same hymn sung in an inner city. We need to bear in mind, too, that hymns not only give us ways to express ourselves to God, but may also form us spiritually and theologically through the act of singing and making them our own.[1] The way in which hymns describe the city, and life in the city, is significant in our spiritual formation.

Hymns express what we believe about the city, and here there is a deep ambivalence within the biblical and Christian tradition. The city is never all good or all bad. Some writers see it almost entirely negatively;[2] others see more hopeful signs and view the city as a place of sanctuary and justice;[3] still others affirm, perhaps too easily, the secular city.[4] We should not be surprised to find the same range of views within hymnody. There are hymns *about* the city and there are hymns *for* the city, hymns that people living there might (or might not!) want to sing to articulate their own situation to God, whether it is one of praise, distress or confusion. Congregations will resist hymns that do not reflect their own understanding of their life. In worship, if a hymn is not for us (even though it may unsettle us), then its value in our worship and spiritual formation must be questioned. Do hymns help us to praise God and pray faithfully in the city? How do they give expression to the pastoral needs that walk into church week by week – needs that are perhaps too powerful or too inchoate for our own words, yet can be caught up and articulated in a winsome hymn?

Hymns open us to depths that prose alone cannot reach, and words and music sung to God – however tentatively – can open people to the presence of God's Holy Spirit. Choosing hymns wisely is an immense pastoral responsibility. Well-chosen hymns should help us to live more faithfully in the here and now, setting our daily experience in the theologically wider context of God's ways with the world and engaging us in a dialogue with God. Yet the indexes of too many books about urban issues make no mention of hymns, and they are noticeably absent from Church reports on the city, as if they have no contribution to make to the life of urban churches.

## The city in hymns

The roots of hymns about the city lie in nineteenth-century hymns that addressed issues such as slavery, temperance and war. It was these hymns that dared to give voice, in worship or in meetings, to issues that affected the social life of the nation, and thus to life in the cities that were growing so rapidly.

Given the slums and the appalling conditions in so many Victorian cities, it is not surprising that the image of the city in hymns from this period is almost entirely negative. A typical phrase from one of the better-known hymns paints a picture of the city as a crowded, raucous place dominated by sin, inhabited by weary, oppressed people:

> Still the weary folk are pining
> For the hour that brings release;
> And the city's crowded clangour
> Cries aloud for sin to cease[5]

And the God who can deal with this is the judge, throned in splendour, to whom we plead for powerful, decisive action. The verbs are telling: purge, crown, cleave, cleanse. Only 'solace' has any sense of comfort. God is active; we are passive and in darkness. Another hymn from this period, 'King of the City Splendid',[6] contrasts the 'City splendid eternal in the height' with our own cities, asking:

> May all our country's cities
> Be holy in Thy sight:
> Cleansed from the deeds of darkness –
> Cities of light.

Cities, in this hymn, are places where children do not laugh and have no rights, where there is no beauty but 'spells of passion', drunkenness and foul life. Yet the petition is for joy, gladness, healing and hope, and the vision is of a well-ordered, glorious city. There is a sense that the city could be a place of community and encounter with God, even though it is now a deathly slum; it is not beyond redemption, and there is hope for a better life within the urban world. Thus the hymn ends:

Give joy to all the joyless,
Song's voice to sorrows dumb,
May light invade with blessing
Each dark and deathly slum;
Into earth's realms of horror
Thy kingdom come!

Soon may our country's cities
Thy robe of glory wear;
Each place of toil a Temple,
Each house a home of prayer;
Each city's name of beauty –
The Lord is there!

A fascinating text dating from 1888, originally published in a book called *Songs of Labour*, epitomizes many of the issues surrounding hymnody and the city, both when it was written and in 1925, when the editors of *Songs of Praise* included it in that hymnal. It is worth quoting in full as it appeared in 1925:

England arise, the long, long night is over,
Faint in the east behold the dawn appear;
Out of your evil dream of toil and sorrow
Arise, O England, for the day is here!
From your fields and hills,
Hark the answer swells:
Arise, O England, for the day is here!

People of England! All your valleys call you,
High in the rising sun the lark sings clear:
Will you dream on, let shameful slumber thrall you?
Will you disown your native land so dear?
Shall it die unheard,
That sweet pleading word?
Arise, O England, for the day is here!

Forth then, ye heroes, patriots and lovers,
Comrades of danger, poverty and scorn,

Mighty in freedom, your great mothers,
Giants refreshed in joy's new rising morn!
Come, swell the song,
Silent now so long:
England is risen! And the day is here![7]

As printed here, there is no mention of the city (or even God). The call is to England and the dominant imagery is rural and idyllic – the call and the answer lie in fields and hills, in the rising sun and the lark singing. In contrast to this, toil and sorrow are but an evil dream from which heroes, patriots and lovers will arise to bring in the day. It is stirring stuff, although the causes of the problems against which England must arise are not spelt out; nor, indeed, is what England will do when it has arisen. However, there are two missing verses, about which the editors of *Songs of Praise* wrote:

> Two stanzas are omitted which the author always preferred to have included; but although they are still, alas, not without truth, recent reforms have already done much, and so much more improvement is being accomplished that even now they begin to appear forced and unreal, which they certainly were not when they were written.[8]

The omitted stanzas (the second and fourth) are:

By your young children's eyes so red with weeping,
By their white faces aged with want and fear,
By the dark cities where your babes are creeping,
naked of joy and all that makes life dear;
From each wretched slum
Let the loud cry come;
Arise, O England, for the day is here!

Over your face a web of lies is woven,
Laws that are falsehoods pin you to the ground,
Labour is mocked, its just reward is stolen,
On its bent back sits Idleness encrowned.

How long while you sleep
Your harvest shall It reap?
Arise, O England, for the day is here.


The city is a place of white people (in contrast to recent hymns
that refer to the racial mix of cities), and the adjective 'dark',
which appears in almost every Victorian hymn about the city,
is again employed to describe the city, while 'Idleness' is capi-
talized, and thus personified, in lines 4 and 6 of the fourth
verse. These two missing verses supply the lacking information
about why England must arise – the answer is the social conditions of the cities and the exploitation of workers. Despite the
flowery language, the specificity of these omitted verses contrasts markedly with the generality of the others. It was true
that conditions had improved enormously since the Victorian
period – the series of Public Health, Housing, Town Planning
and Social Security Acts in the early twentieth century had
secured vast improvements in some areas – but was it really
true in 1925, the year before the General Strike, and of enormous labour unrest, that verses tackling urban poverty were
obsolete while the rest of the hymn was not? Or was the omis-
sion a sign of reluctance to face, in our hymnody, the specificity
of the needs of our urban life?

In these hymns, the solution to the city's problems is decisive action: the city is a problem to be addressed, to be acted
on externally, and the implication is that God is essentially
outside it. In contrast to this, an American hymn from 1903
anticipates encounters with God within the city, in its noise
and strife:


When cross the crowded ways of life,
Where sound the cries of race and clan,
Above the noise of selfish strife
We hear thy voice, O Son of Man.

In haunts of wretchedness and need,
On shadowed thresholds dark with fears,
From paths where hide the lures of greed,
We catch the vision of thy tears . . .

. . . O master, from the mountain side
Make haste to heal these hearts of pain;
Among these restless throngs abide,
O tread the city's streets again:

Till sons of men shall learn thy love,
And follow where thy feet have trod;
Till glorious from thy heaven above,
Shall come the city of our God.[9]

Although God will be met in the city, the implication is that the mountainside is God's home, and the city – a place of wretchedness and need, temptation and sorrow – is a place God will visit. Yet this hymn, written by a minister in New York who was familiar with its life, affirms the city as a place where God is present amid the need. Another from this period, 'The founders built this city',[10] encourages good citizenship in the city of families, this commonwealth of people working together for the good of all, and challenges city-dwellers to praise God. Thus, in two of the verses:

Yet still the city standeth
A busy place as then,
And parents' love makes happy home
For children yet again;
O God of Ages, help us
Such citizens to be
That children's children here may sing
The songs of liberty.

Let all the people praise thee,
Give all thy saving health,

Or vain the worker's strong right arm
And vain the banker's wealth;
Send forth thy light to banish
The shadows and the shame,
Till all the civic virtues shine
Around our city's name.

The 1921 hymn 'When through the whirl of wheels, and engines humming'[11] uses the imagery of industry and the mines to explore God's presence in the industrial context, as well as seeing signs of eschatological hope. It sees in the industrial processes a reflection of God's boundless energy, and its conclusion, that God will again be seen in a workman's jacket, sweeping the workshop floor, is a powerful linking of the carpenter's shop at Nazareth with the 1920s industrial city. It does not comment on the conditions of employment, but in terms of affirming for hymn-singers that their daily work is not God-forsaken, and thus can be the stuff of worship, it is a prophetic voice for its time.

Another hymn, 'God of the pastures, hear our prayer',[12] starts by referring to fields and farmland, but moves on to dark and sombre mines, then the city's throbbing heart. It uses all these locational examples as prompts for a petition. We singers are not necessarily in these locations; they are stated as being God's, and if we reflect on them, we will know what to pray. The rural or urban location is essentially a didactic tool, not a place from which we sing. It was left to a children's hymn[13] in a 1951 Methodist school hymn book to revel unashamedly in the town as a joyful place of bright buses and twinkling street lights, of sparrows and seagulls, friendly people, and noises from hooters, sirens and clocks. Children's hymns are consistently most attentive to the details of life; hymns for adults are often so general that the vibrancy is lost. Even amid this hymn's celebration of the city, however, there is also a commitment to be working actively towards making the city pleasing to God.

In 'God of concrete, God of steel',[14] published in 1958 in
*The Boys' Brigade Hymn Book*, the city is not specifically mentioned, but we are clearly in an urban world of pylons, pistons,
girders, motorways and scientific research. There is no engagement with any of these, and no value judgment of their rightness or wrongness: they are simply listed as things over which
God is Lord. There is no petition in this hymn; instead, the
hymn affirms for the singers that all the world, including the
urban and scientific world, is God's. We are spectators looking
at a city of concrete (prefabricated tower blocks were the new
solution to the housing crisis) and motorways (the M1 was
under construction), and observing a technological world. The
city is not a place of people, but a built environment. Gone is
the throbbing heart and even the crowded clangour: this is a
silent world, almost a ghost city.

Things moved rapidly from the 1960s onwards, when new,
often vivid, images were explored. Thus, one hymn refers to
international time zones in cities such as London, New York,
Toronto and Mandalay;[15] homelessness appears as a theme in
a carol for an urban youth group's Christmas play at the time
when *Cathy Come Home* shocked the nation and Shelter was
founded;[16] the freedom marches in the USA lead to reflection
on racial justice;[17] council flats become the place from which
to sing 'Magnificat';[18] and Jesus Christ is to be found waiting,
raging, healing, dancing and calling in the streets, facing lone-
liness, injustice, suffering and hatred, and calling us to walk
with him.[19] Fred Kaan even parodied the hymn 'City of God'
with his provocative and thoughtful 'City of man, how rich
and right outspread your streets and squares'.[20]

The publication of *Hymns of the City* in 1989 (republished
in 1998) gave us a collection of mainly contemporary hymns
that specifically engage with the city, drawing it into our worship and giving voice to some of the positive, as well as negative,
aspects of city life.[21] It describes itself as a book from and for
small congregations in inner-city and housing-estate churches,

with hymns 'about real people's experiences and not endless "Praise" for no particular reason, as seems to be the custom of the affluent churches'.[22] Some examples from this book show how far, and how fast, hymnody has developed in not only mentioning but wrestling, theologically and spiritually, with urban life. Unlike 'God of concrete', these cities are inhabited, they are communities, vibrant – for good or ill – and they are the subject matter for praise and prayer. Thus, 'Dear God of town and city'[23] paints a picture of a city of buildings, people, roads and roadworks, feelings, events and actions. This is a city of life, and that life is the food for prayer and praise:

Dear God of town and city,
We offer praise to you
From houses, flats, bedsitters
Our thanks we bring anew.
With varied feelings merging
In one great song of praise,
Glad now we stand before you,
Hear, God, the hymn we raise.

You are the God of cities,
And all that happens there.
The God of shop and office
Of store and thoroughfare;
Your love surrounds the theatre,
The hostel and the inn,
Construction sites and roadworks,
Your voice, in all the din.

You are the God of music,
Of hospital and home,
Of factory and town hall,
Of parkland where we roam;
Your judgment is on all things,
On pride and cruel deed,

On those who still cheat others,
On people deaf to need.

Dear God of every city,
Our lives shall offer praise;
We show your love in action
In many varied ways,
Your purpose still invites us,
Your common wealth to share,
And justice, peace and caring
Shall show your presence there.

Like 'God of concrete, God of steel', this hymn affirms that
God is God of the city, and it spells out many of the elements
of urban life. It goes, however, a stage further than the earlier
hymn, and thereby makes itself more useful as a hymn, because our voice is heard. It is a hymn that an urban congregation could sing at the start of worship, as a gathering of all
their life, or later as an act of dedication before they go back
into the city.

'Yours the city, yours the city'[24] also begins with the affir-
mation that the city is God's, and in the second line, makes a
link with Jesus' experience.[25] Structurally, it has much in common with 'God of concrete', in that it lists what is God's. This,
however, is a city of people, not buildings, and the address is
clearly personal to God as 'You', not the more distancing 'God
of'. The hymn blends theological and contemporary connections, alluding to Rastas and the beatitudes within three lines;
and the last verse engages with the Christian tradition as it
explores biblical and eschatological themes:

Yours the city, yours the city,
With no place to lay your head.
Yours the courage, yours the pity,
Yours the life among the dead.

Yours the poor, and yours the beaten,
Struggling to reclaim their rights.
Yours the victimised we threaten,
Seeking allies for their fights.

Yours the claimant, yours the homeless,
Unemployed or underpaid.
Yours the children, desperate, powerless,
Yours the bleeding heart betrayed.
Yours the hopes by cities heightened,
Rastas, pop groups, youth in quest.
Yours the rich, though unenlightened
By the poor you make the blest.

Yours the movement for empowering,
Yours the kingdom, sure and meek,
Yours the banquet for our flowering,
Yours the shalom cities seek.
Ours your faithful love upholding,
Ours your grace outpassing fears,
Ours the mystery unfolding –
Christ who wipes away all tears!

Other hymns from this collection refer variously to reckless drivers dodging through traffic queues, racism, burglary, graffiti, overflowing litter bins, roadworks, construction sites, muggings, dole queues, broken lifts, buses that are late, red tape, fear of strangers and lack of playgrounds. In their attention to the detail of city life, they are the heirs of the children's hymn quoted earlier. Many of these texts tend to address God briefly, then focus on the urban issues, piling on the images and only then addressing them theologically. Yet they provide a lively source of material that forbids us to keep God at arm's length from the city, or to keep God out of the conversation about the trials and tribulations, joys and sorrows, of urban life. In that sense, they have much in common with the Psalms: instead of rocks, we have tower blocks; instead of enemies, we have burglars; instead of green pastures, we have urban parks; and instead of the lute and harp, we have steel bands and reggae music.

## *Using Hymns about Cities*

On the whole, these hymns have, as yet, not made the transition from a book of hymns specifically about the city, which is likely to have limited circulation in most churches, to mainstream hymn books. The texts are, however, there, and are more likely to be of use, spiritually, to urban churches than many of the earlier ones. Most new denominational hymn books include some hymns that bring contemporary life, including the city, into our praise and prayer, and most have a good theological balance between the earlier emphasis on the sin and suffering of the city – a theme most city residents bring to worship,[26] and a perspective we should not lose if the message of prophets is to be heard – and the more hopeful and vibrant perspective of recent texts. But even if hymns are in books, are they used? Are congregations encouraged to sing of the city? On the whole, we are much more comfortable mentioning the city in our spoken intercessions than we are singing about it to God. Is the city even thought of as a subject for the poetry and creativity of hymnody, or is it just a subject for prose? To help a congregation make that shift in thinking could open up new possibilities for envisioning and expressing the concerns of the city.

Few recent resources emerging from the charismatic strand of the Church refer to urban life, at least not in very specific ways. There certainly are texts that refer to cities and nations, often with an overshadowing theme of judgment and the need for repentance that is remarkably similar to that of some of the Victorian texts. As in some of the earlier texts, the onus is on God to act decisively, and we are relatively passive in our engagement with the city. Thus, 'O Lord, the clouds are gathering'[27] refers to impending judgment, to children starving, war threatening and streets flooded with hate and fear, while 'Desolate cities, desolate homes'[28] is a plea for God to act. The petitions are for mercy and revival, for justice to flow and for God's kingdom to come. Except for the fact that they are not written with the strict rhyme and metre of traditional hymnody, they could almost have been written a century earlier. Their author, Graham Kendrick, is one of the few people writing for this tradition who mentions cities in his texts; his 'Beauty for brokenness'[29] is rare in its reference to the biblical concept of cities of sanctuary.

Many songs in contemporary worship books celebrate the goodness of God and joy in worship. Yet these joyful texts are usually decontextualized: our joy does not arise from or within the details of our daily life, let alone city life, so much as from spiritual joy at what God has done for us in Christ. References to the physicality of our world are noticeably absent; an urban congregation using these resources regularly would probably struggle to realize that the ins and outs of daily life in the city can be mentioned in worship, can actually be food for prayer and theological reflection.

It is interesting to reflect that nineteenth-century Ritualist churches in inner-city areas deliberately aimed to create an atmosphere that was a foretaste of heaven – with sights, sounds, smells, colour and ritual to lift the urban poor out of the bleakness of factory and slum life, giving them a brief taste of the joy that is to come, a sense that this world and its suffering is not all there is. Hymns helped with this creation of an atmosphere of 'worship in the beauty of holiness', to which people – whether the urban poor or the clergy and monastics who lived and worked among them – could bring their 'burden of carefulness' and find their sorrows comforted.[30] It was a deliberate pastoral strategy within the liturgy. Is that so different, at least in outward form, from the practice today of using worship songs and hymns to create an atmosphere of worship that aspires to bring us into God's presence, focusing on God's glory and prostrating ourselves in the face of God's holiness? One question about the spirituality of these different approaches must be to what extent daily life has a place in worship: is it to be left behind when gathering to worship, or incorporated? How did, and do, hymns and worship songs form city-dwellers spiritually? What is the situation today, where congregations' joy and sorrow is often expressed in the more abstract language of salvation? Are people able to bring city life to worship, or is it left at the door, to be resumed later?

On the other hand, if hymns are only about our life in the city, where is the bigger theological picture? Where is the message of salvation? Is urban life the only thing we express to God? Are the gospel and worship only about our daily life, in its misery and mirth? Inevitably, the plea must be for hymns that bring all of life, including city life, faithfully and not stereotypically into the heart of worship, so that what happens at school, or in the street on Saturday night, has a place when we come before God in church on Sunday, and our worship can raise theological and pastoral questions about the city.

We neglect the power of hymns at our peril, power exercised both by what they do say and what they don't say – either individually or as a set of hymns sung in a particular service. A well-chosen hymn can have far more effect than the words of the dismissal in getting people out of church and into mission in the world; an appropriate hymn can have more pastoral power than some sermons, and most hymns can go on giving usable words and music for personal prayer throughout the week. How we articulate city life in hymns is a crucial spiritual matter for the Church today. Mercifully, we have come a long way since the following verse was often omitted from

Victorian hymn books for being out of place in a Christmas carol:

> Where children pure and happy
> Pray to the blessed Child,
> Where misery cries out to thee,
> Son of the mother mild;
> Where charity stands watching
> And faith holds wide the door,
> The dark night wakes, the glory breaks,
> And Christmas comes once more.[31]

# 4

## Living in knowable communities

### Leslie Griffiths

◆

'London's a wonderful place,' said Bob Hope, 'or at least it will be when it's finished.' But London will never be finished. It's an organic, developing and dynamic city. And that's precisely what makes it such a wonderful place. London has colour and life. Its grand buildings, sense of history, street markets, carnival, clubs and theatre, parks and pageantry are unrivalled anywhere. Yet there is more. Over and beyond all the monuments and great events are its people; people of all shades and hues, shapes and sizes, futures and backgrounds. I have only to think of the amazing diversity of neighbours I have had since living in London: white East Enders, Greeks and Jews; Arabs and Africans, people of Bangladeshi and Caribbean origins, the lot; and I can testify that this broad spectrum of people is London's supreme glory, its most precious asset and the key element of any vision we may form for the kind of city we want to live in.

People are first of all human beings. They want to lead decent lives, to bring their children up in security, to conduct themselves with integrity. To do this, they need space to be themselves, to think as well as act. They also need an environment that encourages them to build relationships and form communities. City-dwellers are often thrown into proximity with people, a situation that is hardly helped by the high population turnover. This can make 'knowable communities' difficult to establish. 'London appears not to see itself,' said Thomas Hardy[1]. 'Each individual is conscious of himself, but nobody conscious of themselves collectively.' That may be overstating things, but we all know what he meant. Many of us will have lived on streets where we never even got to know the people living next door. The kind of housing we live in sometimes militates against any desire we may have to be part of a community. High-rise flats, forbidding terraces, select and private detached houses: all present difficulties when it comes to encouraging people to be conscious of themselves collectively.

London's development over the centuries has seen the growth of 'villages', knowable communities, indeed, which are scattered throughout the metropolis. I and my family have lived in some of them – Marylebone, Golders Green, Camberwell, Chiswick, Brixton and Islington – and all are as different from each other as chalk and cheese. Yet each offers a model of how people can enjoy a sense of place that strengthens their identity. What is more, London's villages can contribute to the privacy of their inhabitants without losing this sense of community. And both these dimensions need to be cultivated.

We are all individuals, but we are also gregarious creatures. We need each other to survive; we need to be able to recognize and greet people, to pursue matters of common interest with each other and to develop simple support and mutual help systems together. Housing, social services, cultural and community centres, security, access to primary and secondary healthcare, education, work, and all other matters that touch on people's basic needs should always be provided in a way that reinforces the fundamental yearning we all have to live in knowable communities – what the architect Richard Rogers[2] has called 'diverse and compact urban neighbourhoods'. This would make a material contribution to the social environment within which people seek to establish responsible lives. It is, after all, our context that gives us a sense of well-being and self-confidence. A moral or spiritual agenda for city-dwellers cannot be defined simply by the obligation of individuals to lead good lives. Morality isn't simply about the choices people make; nor is spirituality merely a matter of saying our devotions or discovering a sense of the numinous. Everything that shapes people's attitudes and arouses their feelings, the environment that enfolds them and, knowingly or not, shapes and colours their general outlook on life – all this impinges on people's spiritual well-being. Responsible choices are generally made by those who feel secure and reasonably content. Helping people feel safe should therefore be an overriding priority for our social planners and theorists, for those who are responsible for law and order, and for both local and national politicians. If we are to invoke that well-worn cliché 'back to basics', then security has, in my view, to be our number-one priority, a necessary prerequisite for any discussion of a moral or spiritual agenda for city living.

We cannot shut our eyes to the fact that cities in general, and London in particular, have a downside. They offer a refuge for wickedness and squalor, dehumanizing (and therefore immoral) forces that have blighted the lives of innumerable people. London produced Jack the Ripper and the Kray twins, cruel criminals who have become part of its folklore. People go on themed walks to connect with their stories. London is also the city of Stephen Lawrence and Damilola Taylor, whose tragic deaths still cast a deep shadow over the metropolis and its institutions. Dickens[3] described the 'Vice and Fever which propagate together [in London], raining down tremendous social retributions.' It is a depiction that still has the ring of truth about it.

A highly influential pamphlet in late-Victorian times, a seminal document written by Andrew Mearns, a Congregational churchman, and W. C. Preston, called on all responsible people to heed *The Bitter Cry of Outcast London*.[4] I once ran the Methodist Church's West London Mission with a substantial programme of social work directed towards the single homeless, people with addictions and those in trouble with the law. The foundation of that mission, and others like it, was a direct response to the stirring of the national conscience that followed that particular late-nineteenth-century publication. In more recent times, the devastation of a world war, rent racketeering, a shortage of affordable housing, fast-rising unemployment (there were more than 400,000 jobless people in the metropolitan area at one time in the early 1980s), a lack of adequate investment in the city's infrastructure, huge demographic shifts, an overall decline in population and many other factors have conspired to ensure that the problematic side of living in the city has long outlasted the time of Dickens.

Peter Townsend's meticulous study of *Poverty and Labour in London* was written in the 1980s.[5] It is still worth reading. It referred again and again to 'multiple deprivation' and showed how life expectancy and levels of poverty varied from borough to borough, sometimes alarmingly so, and always in relation to the adequacy (or inadequacy) of social provision. More recently, it has become fashionable to speak the language of 'exclusion' rather than deprivation, a welcome concentration on people's need to participate in society, rather than on the goods and chattels they are supposedly lacking. Yet the idea behind both metaphors is the same: too many people are carrying burdens so heavy that they are effectively cut off from the possibility of developing their full potential and participating in those knowable communities, which offer a bulwark against spiritual, as well as economic, impoverishment.

Hanif Kureishi is, in some ways, a contemporary Dickens. The pictures he paints in his novels and television dramas often highlight racism, social disintegration and street violence, a subculture of unrooted and vulnerable people dependent on drugs and casual relationships, all these being some of the main ingredients in the lives of a significant number of people, the shadow side of the hedonistic culture of better-off people, whose own addictions are lavish holidays, sumptuous lifestyles and crazy workloads.

The Christian Church has addressed these questions again and again. It has done so in a non-sectarian way, calling on people of goodwill (whether Christians, members of other faith groups or people with no religious faith at all) to recognize the symptoms of our ailing cities and to acknowledge the ways in which spirituality can be fostered and safe space created for the development of a spiritual agenda.

David Sheppard's *Built as a City*[6] was published as long ago as 1974, on the eve of his departure from London to become Bishop of Liverpool. He drew on 20 years of pastoral experience in the Docklands in his attempt to establish a framework for theological reflection. He recognized the factors that create alienation among city-dwellers, and he admitted the failure of the Church 'to establish a strong, locally rooted Christian presence' there, especially among the groups that society leaves without voice or power. Too often, 'it has only succeeded in reflecting society's fatalism and withdrawal'. With that general point in mind, he sets out to make the case for a way of presenting good news in a context where people know the reality of 'enslavements' to factors that he spells out at length. He analyses the processes and the fact of urbanization in some detail. He looks at the provision of education and other services within the city and highlights the way this, effectively done, can contribute to the general well-being of whole communities. He also examines the nature of power and powerlessness.

In an epilogue to his book, Sheppard argues against simply coming to terms with some patterns of urban community, 'because when we look at them carefully we shall see that they are expressing non-community and non-life'. He argues for a city where healthy relationships can flourish, where social and urban planning allows people to be people, families to be families, neighbours to be neighbours. In the urban jungle, the toughest commodity is love. 'Life comes through our smaller "deaths", as it does through His Cross'; and good communities, knowable communities, will require the best efforts of those who live on our streets as well as those who plan the environment we live in. In Sheppard's view, 'we must hold on to the dream that it is possible for a place to be built as a city, and to know, in the thick of its life, good and life-sustaining relationships between each other and with God.'

The early 1980s saw violence erupt on the streets of many British cities, signs of deep-seated unrest, particularly on the part of ethnic minorities. A fire in New Cross, south-east London, in January 1981 revealed an ugly situation just waiting to explode: 13 young people died at a birthday party, a tragedy that had all the marks of a racially motivated attack, although nobody seemed to (want to) take any notice. The police, the Establishment, the press and the general public simply ignored it. But for black people, this could not be overlooked. Thousands of them marched into central London in a demonstration that surprised everyone, including themselves. Their questions appeared on the front pages of our newspapers for the first time, though in a hugely distorted and negative way. Later that same summer, riots in Brixton, Toxteth, Handsworth, Moss Side, Leeds and Bristol shook smug British society to its roots. Something had to be done; it was no longer enough to sweep the problems of multiracial Britain under the carpet.

The Church of England marshalled its forces, once again under the leadership of David Sheppard, and in 1985 issued a report on what it chose to call 'urban priority areas'. *Faith in the City*[7] caused a considerable stir, and was dismissed by many prominent people in a Conservative government at the zenith of its power as a left-wing and seditious document. Soon, however, responsible theologians were mounting a rearguard action, a keen defence of the report. Anthony Harvey edited a volume of essays called *Theology in the City*,[8] which took a serious look at various kinds of local or 'bottom-up' theologies emerging from the city. Liberation and black theology were examined to see whether, and how, their insights could help in the attempt to understand and address the needs of our troubled cities. It was time, wrote Andrew Kirk, one of the contributors, 'to give every encouragement to the growth of theologies that are authentic expressions of local cultures'.

The search for a new way of doing theology is intimately linked to the question of the quality of life. It prioritizes the poor, but not simply by defining poverty in materialistic terms. It reminds us of how 'the Bible lays tremendous emphasis on interpersonal and community relationships. Where these are in disarray, particularly regarding the fundamental relationship with God, there is abject human poverty, or absence of *shalom*.' A 'quality of life' criterion will also need to be applied to the provision of healthcare, with 'human wholeness' set as the objective. And there is room, argues Kirk, 'for a good deal of reflection on the meaning of human wholeness, and in what ways the local Christian community can see part of its task as creating a greater awareness of the spiritual, moral and physical integrity of human beings in situations of deprivation'.

At the heart of this little volume lay Andrew Hake's chapter, 'Theological Reflections on "Community"'. Hake recognizes the fact that the word 'community' can be a weasel word, 'an aerosol word, popularly sprayed into discussions, giving a sweet scent and a hint of mist, clouding analysis'. He regrets the fact that the word conjures up so many competing definitions. 'But,' he avers, 'all exist within the general framework of a discussion of personal relationships between human beings in groups, in society, and in the total "human community".'

He goes on to address the issue of pluralism, arguing that it suggests far more than merely ethnic diversity. The big question is: 'How can incompatibilities coexist?' Those who live in our cities are surrounded by deep differences in culture and religion; there is a plurality of lifestyles, ethical norms and ideologies. We are therefore forced to ask ourselves whether 'the universe coheres in an ultimate unity or whether we're in a "polyverse" with no integrating principle'.

There is so much of value in this collection of essays that should continue to stimulate discussion in our postcolonial, postmodern age. Over and above all, however, is the inevitable linkage, spelt out again and again, between the social environment where people live and their own need to discover and enjoy their inner integrities. 'Living in knowable communities', while not a phrase used in this volume, seems again and again to be the presupposed principle underlying the social, political, psychological, theological and spiritual search for a sense of well-being within the city.

Less well known, perhaps, is 'A Vision for London', the subtitle of a special issue of the *Christian Action Journal* published in 1990.[9] That particular vision identified three strands to the moral and spiritual dimension of any visionary hope we may form for the city:

1 Spiritual values: the provision of an environment which allows people to enjoy a true sense of their worth;
2 Human dignity: the creation of a context that offers a firm and fair framework for people's everyday lives;
3 Social justice: the enactment of public policies, properly monitored, so that the squalid conditions in which a substantial minority of London's population lives can be countered systematically and with conviction.

This report, the product of the brilliant and late-lamented Christian Action – a theological think-tank directed by Eric James, whose main focus was on a social and political agenda – spoke of the disintegration of the fabric of London, the impoverishment of its healthcare facilities, the deterioration of its housing stock, a decaying transport system, crumbling infrastructure and rampant (the Lawrence inquiry had not yet given us the adjective 'institutional') racism. There has, of course, been a significant attempt to reverse the long years of underinvestment in London's infrastructure. This has sometimes felt, to use the graphic words of a well-known politician, like pouring water into sand. It is sad to think that the context within which Londoners made their choices and endeavoured to live decent lives was for so long deprived of a London-wide strategic authority. The absence of such a body for a whole decade, following the destruction of the Greater London Council (GLC) in the mid 1980s, led to the disintegration of a vital commitment to address the needs of citizens on a metropolitan scale. Among those pleading for a far more devolved approach to social and urban planning was Michael Parkinson (formerly director of the European Institute for Urban Affairs in Liverpool), who appealed for a reversal of what he called the 'castration' of local government's powers. The heavy hand of centralization, he argued, needs to be relaxed in favour of far more powerful regions, able to respond to the economic, social, cultural (and, I'd add, moral and spiritual) needs of ordinary people. As far as London was concerned, Richard Rogers pointed out that the responsibilities of the former GLC had come to fall between five government departments, 33 London boroughs, the City of London and some 60 committees and quangos. The first modern European capital to have an elected government authority became the only such city without one.

It is good to note a significant reversal of this trend. The Welsh Assembly and the Scottish Parliament have seen real power devolved away from Whitehall. The Greater London Assembly and the Mayor of London are now able to bring a sense of coherence back to our capital city.

The Christian Church, recognizing the secular and pluralistic times in which we live, must commit itself to staying in the city, in solidarity with all those who live there, especially with its poorest and most disadvantaged inhabitants. It hasn't always been good at this. David Sheppard quoted the comment of a London dock worker to a priest who had spent three years in a beat-up inner-city parish. 'I suppose you'll be off soon,' he said ruefully, 'just like the rest of them.' This view is echoed in the pretty standard advice that bishops used to use to address new incumbents. 'Don't bury yourself,' they would say. 'Keep in touch, and we'll find you something in about five years' time.' For 'something', read 'something better'.

Mercifully, such attitudes are now, at last, changing, and the Church is finding ways of recommitting itself to the inner city. Indeed, the Church is there on the ground in every London borough; it can put its finger on the city's pulse and speak with authority about the lives Londoners live; and it cannot, simply cannot, be left out of any process that envisages the social, economic, moral or spiritual health of the metropolis. I do not, of course, mean that the Church has any right to impose its particular belief system on anyone; it must be ready to work with people of goodwill, whatever their class, colour or creed. There must be a readiness to respond to the needs of the socially excluded, the weak and the marginalized. There must be a commitment to campaigning for justice and fairness in all sectors of the city's life, whatever accusations of partisan-ship might be engendered by such a readiness to speak out and act for particular points of view. There must, equally, be a preparedness, as Michael Parkinson put it, to cherish our cities and invest more in them. They are vibrant places with the potential for success and great creativity, the real wealth of our nations. Yet wealth, at the end of the day, cannot be measured simply by money. It has far more to do with people's sense of purpose and their willingness to contribute creatively to the common good. Harnessing the energies and goodwill of ordinary people is what real wealth-creation is all about. The spiritual well-being of London's future is directly related to precisely this understanding of its wealth.

I realize that an essay like this, in a volume that purports to discuss spirituality in the city, may be dismissed as too 'social', or even 'political'. Surely, the argument might run, we needed a discussion of ways to meditate, or we need writers/ thinkers/poets/artists who can provide us with the resources for contemporary life. We need a discussion of 'sacred space' and the relationship between 'being' and 'doing'. We need to know about the discipline of prayer, and it would be helpful if techniques and methods for contemplation were described for us.

And so we do. In agreeing with these desiderata, however, I would still want to justify the need to look at the social context within which spirituality must be fostered. For too long, our approach to the life of the spirit has, subconsciously perhaps, proceeded on a dualistic basis – as if it might be possible to discuss 'spirituality' without considering the environment in which it is to be developed. I would fundamentally reject such an analysis.

When I served as a minister in the Methodist Church of Haiti, I was a member of two of its national committees: the Mission Committee and the Social Responsibility Committee. The Haitian Church was part of the wider Methodist Church of the Caribbean and the Americas, and it had imported its structures from its parent body. As I sat on these two committees, it became obvious to me that my Haitian colleagues were at sea with the agendas facing them. Their reply when I questioned them on the matter was:

> We work at all these questions because we feel the need to behave constitutionally, but we have a profound problem. To have two committees like these, one of them defining matters of faith and the other dealing with social and political issues, seems to us to run counter to our understanding of life. In Haiti, we make no distinction between life and faith, or faith and work, or spiritual and social, or sacred and secular. We'd feel much happier if the work we currently do in these two committees were done in one.

I have never forgotten that holistic approach to life, and any defence I would make for having based this essay on spirituality so squarely in people's social context would make its appeal to the wisdom of some of the poorest people on the face of the earth.

To shape knowable communities where our citizens can live decent and secure lives, and develop their full potential, will undoubtedly be a huge challenge. It will require considerable resources and commitment of a rare kind on the part of planners, politicians and investors alike. In the end, however, its success will lie in the extent to which the visions and dreams we spell out capture the enthusiasm and harness the spiritual energies of the people who live in London. They, when all is said and done, are the city's glory, its life and its very being.

# 5

## Bearing it: the development of a priestly spirituality in Soho

### Clare Herbert

For the past seven years, I have been the Rector of an Anglican church in London's West End. The modern Church and Community Centre of St Anne's, Soho, was built 20 years ago, in a hole created by the bombing in 1940 of the former Parish Church. Perhaps in retreat from the saturation of the senses provided by the life of the surrounding streets, the designers of the modern St Anne's Church made it very plain: light wood panelling and blue and grey colours take you through to a simple garden amphitheatre.

The chapel contains two strong images: a stained-glass window symbolizing St Anne, and a crucifix bearing Christ in metamorphosis towards resurrection. Though I am fond of St Anne, her body containing a meeting – Anne and Joachim, Mary and Gabriel, the Eternal Word and human flesh – the crucifix is the more original work. It is a gift from a family in Germany whose son discovered his vocation to be a priest while living as a student at St Anne's. Jesus looks like a skeletal Jew. He glows, his arms outstretched, imprisoned by his death, skewered by it, bearing it. For me, this Jesus figure has become a model for my priesthood as I struggle to understand it, and a sign of the priesthood of this particular community. It is this priestly spirituality that I shall explore in this chapter.

By the time I arrived in Soho as Rector, two experiences had become etched in my memory. When I was writing my application for the post, quite early one morning, I visited a doctor in Soho Square for treatment for some minor ailment. As I scurried away, back to Trafalgar Square, where I was working at the time, the coffee shops were opening in Soho. Waiters, street cleaners, police and visitors stepped out for a chat; the scent of roasted coffee beans wafted through the air; and I could hear the rustle of newspapers. All this made me think of such things as 'holiday', 'community' and 'village'. I must get this job, I thought, I must, I must; I want to work as a parish priest in an area of the city that still has a strong sense of community! My other memory frightened me like some vision of hell. I had hit Soho late on a Friday night, knowing by now that I had gained the post, and was about to move in. The scene was chaotic: neon colours, psychedelic lights, booming music, drunken and drug-crazed behaviour, broken pavements, huge mounds of litter and, above all, heaving crowds, lurching, pushing and crushing me – what had I done, what had I done? Would I be able to be a priest here? What on earth could I offer?

What I have been learning since those two introductions, one so romantic and one so horrifying, is that neither the romance nor the horror of Soho ever go away. Evil and good exist alongside each other, and they exist in me as well as in the individuals and groups with whom I work. What I have to offer as a priest is the capacity to bear both sides of the paradox of what it is to be human without destroying and excluding, without offering any judgment other than the judgment of love.

A seminal image for me, in the formation of my spiritual life and theology, arises from my life as a childcare social worker. On one training day, I watched a social worker, an expert in child protection, talking with a child. She sat on the floor with the child opposite, both of them concentrating on the space between them, which was full of dolls. As she worked, it seemed to me that she span a circle of safety around the child, the dolls and herself, a circle within which a story could gently unfold. She span this circle unobtrusively, with her manner, her gestures, her words and her quiet authority, but she span it firmly, holding the child in conversation and play. Watching her, I had one of those moments Bishop Ian Ramsey would have called 'penny dropping' or 'eye-opening'. I saw the circle in which I sit with God, praying; I saw the attention with which God holds me; and I saw, too, how useful the experience of social work and counselling could be to me, as my conversation partner with theology, when I entered the Church. I saw the circle of the local church, a safe space, encompassed by a sense of the Holy, in which people can grow in their relationships with God and with one another. I saw the need for someone safe and sure, someone able to bear the tension of those relationships and to interpret them from time to time, someone who could hold the circle together. I saw myself as a priest.

Making a safe space is exactly what I am doing in Soho. It is an amazing place to work. Hardly anyone in the congregation is free of pastoral problems; hardly anyone fits the Church of England stereotypes of successful, let alone holy, human living. We are not very big as a church but, because the level of both need and care is high, the church is well attended. A very large part of my job consists of simply bearing it, of holding the circle together and trying not to be broken myself. I see God holding us there, bearing the paradox of our evil and our good without having to get rid of either; holding us, bearing us and not needing to destroy any part of us. New people move in and out, drawn not to theological statement but to a circle in which they can be held and in which they can grow in the worship of God, in love for each other and in service to the community. Some leave. But who am I to exclude anyone? What would be the purpose of a church for Soho if it were empty of people?

My main effort goes into not falling for the heroic model of priesthood – I don't answer the doorbell all the time and, on a bad day, I hide my entire attention behind the false front of my answering machine. I have time off and take good holidays as far away from Soho as I can. I don't pretend that anyone in the congregation is my particular friend, and I keep a wide circle of space around me, so that all members of the congregation can find me equally accessible; I am not interested in creating a clique around me. I try to let people depend on me, but I try not to let them depend too heavily, except for short periods when they are in particular need. I try to keep hold of my ordinary humanity, because I believe Soho could kill anyone who tried to be heroic on its territory. I try to devolve responsibility among members of the community and to collaborate with colleagues, although I find both difficult. I try to hold the circle.

I try equally hard not to fall for the management model of priesthood. That model, I am sure, is a defence against anxiety, because the aims we strive to achieve are so high that we are bound to fail. Managing my budget at St Anne's means managing a business, the business generated by the Community Centre and its workers. Reliable administrators and care workers are not attracted to living or working in Soho, so any attempt to run a business to pay for my stipend, or to contribute to the wider funds of the diocese, takes on a comic aspect. I am saved any sense of managerial success by confronting, on a daily basis, the image of myself running around bamboo poles, holding up saucers and hearing elderly people say to me: 'Everyone's too busy to visit these days, aren't they dear?' And my hissing back: 'Yesssssssssss.'

Despite all that, despite my resisting the heroic and managerial models of priesthood, I do not fall for the opposite extreme; I don't pretend that anyone could do my job. I know that something very special happens in the Eucharist. No matter how 'outside' I may have been, and am, in a structural and social sense, when I say the Eucharist I am not at all outside. I have never been more inside in my life. The closest

I come to knowing what it means for God to bear us, and the paradoxical nature of our humanity, is in my presidency at the Eucharist.

Before our ordination as women to the priesthood, there was no way of knowing the shocking privilege of celebrating the Eucharist, of praying the Eucharistic prayer, of daily aligning one's being with the story of Christ. Nor was there any way of knowing how much celebrating the Eucharist changes the self of the priest, and involves him or her in the story's dynamic with those around the altar, every time the story is told. I thought I knew what priesthood was – I was already a pastor, a teacher, a preacher of sermons – but I had not expected to have the experience of the sacred, brought to me by saying the Eucharist, so frequently and vividly played out in my life; nor had I expected my role to be, to such an extent, one of mediating that experience of the sacred to others. I sometimes feel as if all the other things I do, from community work to counselling, fade into insignificance when compared to the regular repeating of those words and of that action. Perhaps this is because it is, in Soho, even for one single moment, impossible to maintain the illusion that a church or priest can beat back the waves of evil to form some better territory; perhaps it is because this task seems so impossible that the taking of our suffering and evil, as well as our health and goodness, into the Eucharist for God's holding is especially important to me there. I gain a sense that I am forgiven much by many people because I can do this and can try to live that divine bearing, working always not to reject, but to include and endure.

So far so good, but isn't this all rather Congregationalist? A priest among her people, fine, but what about the whole institution, what about the centre, what about belonging within the hierarchical body, which is the Church of England?

I am ambivalent in my feeling about that wider institution and my belonging there. Of course I am. On the one hand,

I owe it my life, or at least a job: a recognized role within it that, more than any other career I could think of, uses the different fragments of me to the full. On the other hand, it very nearly didn't allow me that: only at the age of 40 did I realize the vocation I had known since I was 17! There were many things I could have done that were quashed by the attitudes of this institution towards women. That gives me a special position, a particular viewpoint with regard to the institution and its centre. I can understand the many people in Soho who feel marginalized because I myself have been an outsider.

Being outside shows you things. One of the things it forces is a realization that priesthood exists outside the Church, because, for us, it had to. I recall Jim Cotter telling me that one way for me to grow, in the 20 years while I waited, was to practise my priesthood – to accept that I could gather people, communicate the word of God with them, pastor them, make liturgies with them and be a space where they might sense a transparency towards the things of God. As time went on and women grew bolder, this became an important method of rebellion. Through the work of the Movement for the Ordination of Women and other groups, liturgies were taking place throughout the country, where women practised their priesthood.

In a less ritualized way, a still more important thing was happening: women were realizing in their ordinary lives that the breaking-open of the holy was happening. William Country-man urges us to begin here in his book *Living on the Border of the Holy*. He writes of a priestly task for all humanity, of break-ing open the new to another, through friendship, parenting, teaching, counselling; and of entering a deeper realm, where that which is communicated is mysterious, not easily defined in human language, let alone in the categories and creeds of religion.[1] When, as a social worker, I worked with families where a child had serious kidney failure, it seemed that the stories people told me as they walked this difficult way were religious, although they did not know this – or that I was a deaconess in disguise. It was probably in those storytelling hours of being a paediatric renal social worker that I most clearly glimpsed the holy tales of all of our lives, and sat with people to form an opening in which meaning could be explored and ritual actions of care and imagination practised.

Just as women discovered that the divine within all things cannot be tied down to the shrine, so they had a place from which to view the male hierarchy of the Church and to learn to be at least partly independent from it. If that hierarchy could be wrong, or unjust, or blind in relation to the priestly vocation of women, it could be wrong about many things; it deserves respect, but it is not safe to hand too much of one's own self-worth over to such as hierarchy. This is a useful lesson in an institution that relies so heavily on secrecy, patronage and indistinct hierarchy. The favour of clergy and bishops is not a good bedrock on which to build a sense of self-esteem or a sense of vocation or direction. We need to set alight that way of valuing ourselves, as do children when growing apart from their parents in order to achieve self-affirmation.

I am always absolutely astonished when someone tells me that they will go wherever a bishop sends them or asks them to go, rather than seeking out a suitable post for themselves. To allow someone to have that much decision-making power over one's health and well-being, for so many years of one's life, strikes me as extraordinary; it reveals an unhelpful, childlike dependence on someone on whom it may be neither safe nor wise to depend. For me, the advertising of all posts is a serious goal to strive for, as it enables clergy to become less dependent, more able to assess their own needs and skills, able to decide, like any adult, as much as they can about their own future.

This sort of attitude towards authority I sometimes find very liberating. I was a curate at St Martin-in-the-Fields at the time of the Lambeth Conference in 2004, with its unhappy ramifications for gay and lesbian people. Several bishops and their wives had already expressed ambivalence towards me as a woman priest when they found out that I was in charge of many services when the vicar was away. I was not, therefore, phased by the results of the conference, but male colleagues, who had quite enjoyed the flurry and fuss of receiving attention from the hierarchy besieging St Martin in the run-up to the conference, seemed stunned, disillusioned and confused by what had happened; their very fathers had let them down. I, however, who had for so long not believed that the hierarchy of the Anglican Church was mercifully paternal, was not unduly perturbed. It has been terribly important to me to free myself from putting too much authority outside myself and into their hands. I work to restore confidence and authority within myself, and to help others find their own sense of authority – authority resides within the self, as I work in the circle. I take dialogue with my bishop very, extremely seriously, but it remains dialogue.

This view provides me with a pastoral method within the parish, and indeed with other structures of the Church. A pastoral letter from the Archbishop of Canterbury was read in the parishes on my first Sunday as Rector of Soho, a letter I could in no way agree with or read out in those early days before anyone could separate me from its contents. The letter needed to be shared and its authority considered. At the end of the service, therefore, I invited the congregation to read it together and, in a safe space, to comment as they wished. We thus discovered our own mind in relation to the mind of the Archbishop and went on from there. I am not a maverick; I take things seriously, but I do not hand over power and insight entirely to another, or expect my parish to do so. I expect my own authority to be taken seriously too, and to have my views considered and reflected on as well.

It does concern me that the centre, and in particular the House of Bishops and the Lambeth Conference of Bishops, do not act like this, and seem to deny the importance of a number of issues. I am genuinely appalled at the lack of women in the most serious decision-making councils of the Church of England. I agree with Penny Jamieson, Bishop of Dunedin, when she writes, in *Living at the Edge*: 'The Christian Church is so imbued with the normativity of male experience that female experience is excluded; in fact it is simply not noticed, and the participation of women makes little difference, is not a focus for analysis or comment.'[2]

I am also worried by the silencing of gay and lesbian clergy. The centre seems to me to be so anxious about disintegration that it has become rigid. It is as if, using my previous analogy, an ogre were sitting in a circle with a child, with the child being firmly controlled not to speak. That sort of over-rigid control leads either to dull submission or to rebellion. Part of a social worker's toolkit is to recognize healthy and unhealthy families – families where members are silenced tend to create the ground where abuse can take place. Families that communicate well, allow all members to speak and have permeable boundaries are more likely to survive healthily, and in these terms of function and dysfunction, we have much to learn in our Church.

In order to manage my own anxieties over these things, I remember the history of our Church and its many periods of rebellion and unrest, indeed of war and strife. Priests often survived by holing up in their own areas, sometimes quite literally, and appearing again in their true colours only when it was safe to do so. But the dividing line between sensible survival and duplicity is, I know, very thin, so I often wonder on which side I fall. How can we, in our priestly formation, grow in inner authority while remaining close to the Christ of the Eucharist, on the one hand, and respecting the authority of the centre on the other? How to hold together obedience and dissent is a vital question for us to address, both in our own personal identity and in our priestly and prophetic role.

Is it, in short, possible to create a spirituality of pastoral care and priestly protest? For me, the sense of God's bearing the fullness of our humanity is just as relevant and important when we talk about the wider institution, as it wrestles with theology. Trying to hold together, in difference, has become an enormous problem within the wider body of the Church, partly because we are no longer trying to bear one another. We axe, we cut and exclude; we warn, we admonish and threaten. For some, that which is female within us all must be devalued; for others, that which is homosexual within us all must be denied. For some, that which is violent within us all must be ignored; for others, that which is vulnerable and frail within us all must be derided. When we make judgments about what is 'inferior' in human nature – and therefore unbearable to us – we turn that supposedly inferior being into a scapegoat, and try to drive it away from us; we develop doctrines of 'taint'; we appoint hierarchs who are 'sound'; we create groups who are 'pure'; and we try to shield parishes and areas, even provinces, from that which is fearful, for no better reason than that it is 'other', even if it is found within our own selves. While we avoid contemplating parts of ourselves, entire sections of our society and, indeed, of the world feel excluded from the spirituality of the Church. Hardly surprising, then, that they look elsewhere for a spiritual path to hold and guide them. God continues to find them, but not through us, and the vibrancy of the Church's life is diminished as our own selves become thinner and less vital.

To be a priest in full-time ministry seems to me to be a powerful role, exciting and exacting, a role of holding both individuals and communities in a circle that is open to God. The role necessarily holds within itself a tendency towards heroism – a heroism that can be dangerous, because it exhausts the body and mind, and betrays the trust of needy folk, who are not helped by our trying to live up to, and beyond, their projections of omnipotence towards us. It holds within itself, too, a temptation to become simply a manager of people, increasing buildings, money and participants because their increase guards us against the fearful thought that we do not know what we are doing.

Women priests might offer a useful critique of this priesthood from the point of view of those who have been outside in the wilderness, unrecognized by the centre. The Church of England in which I grew up managed to listen to its worker priests, its South Bank theologians, its Harry Williams, Monica Furlong and John Robinson, and it had space for a David Randall, a Donald Reeves and an Una Kroll. We women priests may exist in a wilderness even more than they did, as those who surround us speak even less the language of our faith than did those who listened to them. Hence the even greater need to discover our inner faith and authority. You can be especially creative dancing out there on the margins, in the wilderness.

For many people, Soho is synonymous with 'sin'. Since working in Soho, I have come to understand how the area may be used to discard, hide and jettison those parts of our humanity, and of our London life, that we know to exist, but do not wish to own. My formation as a priest owes much to my struggle to love, bear and understand that discarded side of us all, which Soho so vividly represents. To return to the Church of St Anne and my ministry there, I often sit before the crucifix, which bears a tiny leaf. The candlesticks also bear leaves, and so does the font bowl. These were all made by the sculptor Duttenhoeffer. He carved a leaf blowing in the wind of the Spirit from Christ, down through history, and now among those who stand around the symbols of the altar. By the time the wind of the Spirit reaches the font, it has become a storm, and all sorts of human signs are swept around the metal bowl: signs for gender, for learning and for creativity. It is as if the artist is trying to say that Christ redeems and bears all things, all aspects of our human nature. It is the pain of that sort of love that we must learn to bear, a love strong enough to sustain the paradoxical nature of our being without ever giving in to the urge to hate, exclude or destroy.

I am writing a prayer for this Christ, a prayer that I can use in the development of my life in this priestly community:

> Christ, now that I am full,
> I am content to sit before your emptiness.
> How lovely you are, in metamorphosis towards resurrection,
> While I sit in metamorphosis towards life.
> Arms outstretched, you bear all that we give you to bear.
> You are emaciated, racked, aged by that bearing
> Yet not destroyed, alive, glowing, about to fly out of the
>     metal.
> You bear all that we give you to bear
> That, seeing you, we may endure all that is given us to bear
> As we struggle to birth a community
> In metamorphosis towards life.

# 6

## *Cities and human community*

### Philip Sheldrake

—————•◆•————

I want to suggest that the future of human cities and their meaning is one of the most critical spiritual issues of our time. I have to say at the outset that I am not offering solutions. My concern is to provide a perspective. Indeed, it seems to me that what is so often missing from contemporary concerns about cities is precisely a vision. And vision or perspective, rather than some kind of definitive conclusion, is a primary theological task.

At a basic level, environments shape the human spirit and our understanding of what enhances the human spirit shapes the environments we create. In addition, the city in particular has always been a powerful symbol of how we understand 'community', of the overall value we place on community and of the ways in which our communities succeed in being inclusive or not. So, can our future cities reinforce a sense that life itself is 'centred', rather than fragmented? Are we building anything into them that is precious to us? What are the connections between architecture, urban design and spirituality? How can we live spiritually in the city?

Cities are pre-eminently *the* human construction. They represent and create a climate of values that define how we understand ourselves and gather together. Cities also shape our sensibilities and ways of seeing the world. There are four aspects of cities that must be borne in mind. First, we need to hold together the concepts of *urbs* (the physical place, the buildings) and *civitas* (people and their life together). Second, the issues surrounding cities are never purely practical. For example, transportation obviously involves matters of engineering, management, investment and strategy; the balance, however, of private and public transport, say, is also linked to how we understand the common good versus individual choice. Third, the notion of a city is complex, not simple. We cannot separate architecture from urban planning, technology from people, the local from the global. Finally, the meaning of cities must embrace their past if desires for the future are to be fully grounded.

Alongside the well-documented question of an expanding world population lies that of the growth rate of cities. The figures over the past 50 years or so are illuminating. In 1950, 29 per cent of the world's population lived in urban environments. By 1965, this had risen to 36 per cent, by 1990 to 50 per cent. This is likely to rise to somewhere between 60 per cent and 75 per cent by 2025.[1] This makes the meaning of cities one of the most pressing questions that we face. There will never be a single conclusive answer. Indeed, as we shall see, some thinkers, including the French cultural theorist and theologian Michel de Certeau, have argued passionately for resistance to simple attempts at urban systematization and homogenization, which de Certeau saw as destructive. Our attempts, however, to confront the question of the city need to involve much more than economics, engineering, architecture and planning: the city is where, for an increasing proportion of the human race, 'the practice of everyday life' takes place.

For many people, the city is a symbol of social and economic opportunity. For others, the city is a symbol of how our origins, caste and class can evaporate: I can become anything I choose to make myself. Equally, what might be called 'city experience' dominates the culture and thinking of governments, commerce and the media. This dominant culture ensures that groups who do not qualify as urban do not merit the best services – transport, schools, stores, banking or a post office – because they are not deemed viable. For these and other reasons, the question 'What is a city?' becomes philosophical, theological and spiritual, as well as architectural or economic.

## *The crisis of place*

Over the past 50 years or so, Western societies have under-mined place identity in pursuit of values driven largely by eco-nomic considerations. In different contexts, economic and social rationalization has produced contradictory impulses: the centralization of what was once local, and the dispersion to multiple sites of what was once a multidimensional blend of living, working and leisure in a single location. The net effect of this has been a growing emphasis on mobility and the grow-ing relativity of space.[2] 'The skyscrapers, airports, freeways and other stereotypical components of modern landscapes – are they not the sacred symbols of a civilization that has deified reach and derided home?'[3] Indeed, mobility is now under-stood to be a freedom bought by money and education. Re-maining in the same place has come to symbolize a lack of choice, an entrapment, that is the lot of the poor, the elderly and people with disabilities. In an increasingly placeless cul-ture we become 'standardized, removable, replaceable, easily transported and transferred from one location to another'.[4]

The French anthropologist Marc Augé has described what he terms 'non-place'. He distinguishes between place, full of historical monuments and creative of social life, and non-place, where no organic social life is possible. By non-place, Augé means the contexts where we spend more and more time: supermarkets, airports, hotels, motorways, in front of the television, sitting at a computer and so on. These experiences bring about a fragmentation of awareness that leads to in-coherence in relation to 'the world'. Augé describes non-place as 'curious places which are both everywhere and nowhere'. By contrast, 'place' is a concrete and symbolic construction of space that serves as a reference for all those to whom it assigns a position. 'Place' is also a principle of meaning for those who live in it, and a principle of intelligibility for those who observe it. Unlike non-place, 'place' has three essential characteristics – it engages with our identity, with our relationships and with our history.[5]

In a complex study on the social life of cities, Richard Sennett, the eminent American sociologist based at the LSE, blames in part a tendency in Christian theology for the contemporary privatization of space – a process that began several hundred years ago. Essentially, Sennett argues that modern Western culture suffers from a divide between interiority and exteriority: 'It is a divide between subjective experience and worldly experience, self and city.'[6] This divide, according to Sennett, is based on an unacknowledged fear of exposure. Exposure has the connotation of a threat, rather than of the enhancement of life. The result is that, apart from spaces for the celebration of heritage or consumer needs, city design has concentrated on creating safe divisions between different groups of people. Public space thus becomes bland, as its main purpose is to facilitate movement across it, rather than encounters within it.[7] According to Sennett, for the city to recover, the need is for the inherent value of the outer embodied life to be reaffirmed.

Sennett interprets Christianity unequivocally as a religion of pilgrimage and dislocation, rather than placement. For Sennett, Augustine's *City of God* is the classic expression of the triumph of an inner 'city' in search of eternal fulfilment over the human city.[8] Human social places are to be viewed with suspicion. What is most obviously characteristic of these outer places is difference and diversity. Sennett therefore argues that by denying the true value of the outside, theology has underpinned the way that Western culture doubts the spiritual value of diversity. If the ultimate value of the inner life found expression externally, it was in church buildings or in cathedrals. For Sennett, these places actually undermined any meaningful definition of the city in itself.[9] Sennett further suggests that modern urbanism, with its sterile public spaces, stems from what he calls 'a Protestant ethic of space'. This is a further refinement of the Augustinian distinction that he posits. I agree with much that Sennett says concerning urban culture, but his interpretation of Augustine is too sharply drawn. Equally, as I shall mention later, there are other ways of interpreting the role of cathedrals as the historic centres of cities.

Because Augustine's *City of God* was more concerned with the city as community (*civitas*) than as physical place (*urbs*), people have drawn from it a radical distinction between earthly and heavenly cities. The seventh-century bishop Isidore of Seville appeared to reinforce this distinction. He described *urbs* and *civitas*, 'cities of stone; cities of men', as existing on two separate planes, without necessary interaction. Whether this is a fair interpretation of Augustine and Isidore or not – and I don't think it is – the image remained etched in the minds of people until the late Middle Ages and, arguably, into the modern era. In practice, of course, there needs to be a dialectical relationship between the two planes. Only then will there develop a community-centred plan for cities that expresses the ways life is actually lived, or that people hope it may be lived, rather than just some abstract notion of the city determined by 'planners' or urban theorists.

Essentially, the true 'city', for Augustine, was the community of believers that was destined to become the City of God. Clearly, Augustine was rightly suspicious of any attempt by Christian rulers to suggest that their Christian commonwealth was somehow the Kingdom of God. This aspect of Augustine's legacy gives Christianity a great deal of prophetic ammunition to attack any attempt to canonize economic and political systems (for example, capitalism or Marxism–Leninism), or particular empires (such as Hitler's thousand-year Reich). It does, however, leave Christianity weak when it comes to offering positive visions for reconstructing human societies or for

71

reclaiming public places as sacred. This is a legacy that Christianity still struggles to overcome.[10] To be fair, however, the individualism and emphasis on privacy that permeates so much of Western culture would have been alien to Augustine. In his commentary on the book of Genesis, the root of all evil was self-enclosure or privacy. The Heavenly City was to be a community in which the fullness of sharing would be had. For Augustine, it is humanity, rather than autonomous individuals, that is created in the image of God. Virtue consists of defending what is public or held in common. There will be no room in the Kingdom of God for a self-enclosed and protected privacy.[11]

While Augustine's theory of history is eschatological, and the Earthly City is undoubtedly contingent, human history is God's creation and is not to be condemned as merely evil. Augustine's distinction between sacred and secular cities does not render the history of contingent places meaningless. What Augustine rejected was any sense that the contingent world, or human politics, is of ultimate value.

At the start of the eleventh century, when a more organized urban life began to revive and towns to expand for the first time since the end of the Western Roman Empire, two things stand out. First, the urban population continued to need a favourable rural environment, because city-dwellers were great consumers. Medieval cities were still inextricably part of their surrounding landscapes, and the division between urban and rural life was not hard and fast. It is not therefore surprising that in the decoration of medieval cathedrals – Chartres, for example – images of rural life such as the seasons, harvesting and vine-growing predominate. 'The countryside' was not objectified as a place for leisure. In contrast, today's city is essentially disconnected from the surrounding landscape and sources of food production. Citizens today are global consumers, and the supposed limitations of seasonal foods are a thing of the past.

Urban growth in subsequent centuries also led to the development of the notion that 'the city' could be understood as a holy place. Sometimes, this was because of the concentration of religious buildings and artefacts. Italy also defended the ideal that civic life in itself, with its organized community of people living in concord, could be just as much a way to God as monastic life.[12] The city was often seen as an ideal form of social life that was, in effect, an image in this world of the ultimate heavenly Jerusalem. There is a whole medieval literary genre, *laudes civitatis*, poems that articulated a utopian ideal of civic life. This has some interest as, once again, we seek a meaning for the city that is more than pragmatic. Like the glories of the heavenly city, the human city is depicted in the *laudes* as a place where many and diverse people are able to live together in peace. This *pax urbana* is explicitly related to the *pax monastica* that replaced the imperial *pax Romana*. Then cities were renowned for the quality of communal life, in which each and every citizen or group found a particular place that contributed to building up the whole. Finally, medieval cities were regularly praised as places of hard work. The point of mentioning all this is not merely to show, as medieval scholars now emphasize, that holiness in the Middle Ages was not exclusively bound up with monks or clergy, but could be shared by urban communities; the point is also that the city itself was idealized as a utopian vision, with a number of key spiritual qualities.[13]

By contrast, the monumental modernist architecture that still characterizes many of today's cities does not stand for the value of individual people, for intimate relationships or for focused community. Rather, it speaks the language of size, money and power. Commercial complexes such as the Canary Wharf tower, in London's Docklands, exist in brooding isolation rather than in a relationship to anywhere else. Modern cities built in the past 50 years frequently lack proper centres that express the whole life of a multifaceted community. Even the centres of older European cities, reconstructed since the devastation of World War II, can be described as soulless.

A significant part of the problem was the cellular view of urban planning (originating in part from the French architect Le Corbusier), which divided cities into 'special areas' for living, working, leisure and shopping. The immediate consequence was a fragmentation of human living and of a sense of diverse community. On top of this, the creation of a 'city of special areas' has the effect of emptying parts of it at night, especially the centres and commercial districts. This tends to make them dead and even dangerous. Finally, a cellular design demands the separation of areas by distance and clear boundaries. This substantially increases the need for travel, and consequently increases pollution.

In more general terms, this differentiation into discrete areas may be said to reflect a growing secularization of Western culture. There is no longer a centred, not least spiritually centred, meaning for the city. It is now a commodity, fragmented into multiple activities, multiple ways of organizing time and space, matched by multiple roles for its inhabitants.[14] Overall, cellular urban design does not invite people out into shared, humane places of encounter. New domestic ghettos are increasingly protected against sterile public spaces that are no longer respected but, at best, are treated unimaginatively and, at worst, are abandoned to violence and vandalism.

Cities reflect and affect the quality of human relationships. The fact is that in the context of urban environments, we cannot separate functional, ethical and spiritual questions. If places are to be sacred, they must affirm the sacredness of people, community and a human capacity for transcendence. I would argue, against Richard Sennett, that in an earlier age, the cathedral fulfilled that function in European cities. It was at the same time an image of God and a symbol of the ideals of the citizens at the heart of the city.

In a sense, the cathedral offered a focus not simply for a two-dimensional pattern of the city – its static 'map' or 'grid'. There was a third dimension, movement through space, that did not operate merely on the horizontal plane, but also upward. Indeed, the cathedral spoke of a fourth dimension – time, and especially transformation through time. In his writings about an urban aesthetic, the American philosopher Arnold Berleant suggests that the role of the cathedral was as a guide to an 'urban ecology' that contrasts with the monotony of the modern city, 'thus helping transform it from a place where one's humanity is constantly threatened into a place where it is continually achieved and enlarged'.[15]

Such an urban 'centre' offers communion with something that lies much deeper than the need simply for regularity and order in shared public life. Centres should not be purely functional, but evocative. If we leave behind the kind of specialist theological language that we must inevitably use about an explicitly Christian symbol like a cathedral, it is possible to speak more generally of what a cathedral (or other important religious building) can achieve as a heart for the city. For example, it deliberately evokes a vision of the world. It expresses the history of human experience, yet it transcends easy understanding. Perhaps most important of all, it is a repository for the memory and the aspirations of the community, which have been constantly renewed and changed across time. To enter such a building is to enter into communion with centuries of human pains, achievements and ideals. Indeed, the moment a building like a cathedral becomes fixed, rather than something fluid and continually changing, it is a museum rather than a living symbol of the city. If the cathedral presented, in architectural form, a living symbol of the ideals of a community, the question is, what has replaced it in the modern city, now that the dominant social institutions are in the secular sphere? Too often, our contemporary cities no longer have a centred quality, because we have built nothing into them that is precious to us.

It is not unusual to regard the modern city as a purely functional environment. Yet even 'function' involves more than simply practical organization. The issue of space is more than a problem of engineering. Urban space has a great deal to do with the creation of perceptions. The height of the skyscraper does not provide the same kind of elevating moral and spiritual presence as the spire of a cathedral. It speaks, rather, of the impersonal forces of sheer size and domination. If we think of the cathedral less as a container of liturgy, and more as a symbol of human values, such a building suggests that, at best, our sense of place is a sense of the sacred – sacred to people, and sacred in relation to a higher order. The fact that we may find it incongruous to think of our built environments as having a sacred quality merely suggests the degree to which the modern city has signally failed to become precious to its citizens; indeed, has precisely failed, at heart, to create a sense of citizenship, as opposed to a mere sense of residence.

Marc Augé writes about the differences between traditional French towns and the new towns 'produced by technicist and voluntarist urbanisation projects'.[16] Traditional towns have not only aspired to be the centre of somewhere (a region) or something (of gastronomy, for example), but have, since the Middle Ages, developed a monumental centre to symbolize and materialize their aspirations. The smallest of towns and villages boast a *place*, or town centre. These contain the buildings that symbolize authority and meaning, whether religious (the cathedral or parish church) or civil (the *hôtel de ville* or *mairie*), or sometimes a historical monument (for example, the war memorial). These buildings tend to overlook an open space through which many of the cross-town routes pass. The key feature, however, is that such town centres were, and are, active places. People gather there. The leading cafés, hotels or businesses concentrate as close to the square as possible. The problem with the new towns, according to Augé, is that they fail to offer 'places for living'. By 'places for living', he means contexts, places 'where individual itineraries can intersect and mingle, where a few words are exchanged and solitudes are momentarily forgotten, on the church steps, in front of the town hall, at the café counter or in the baker's doorway'.[17]

## Resistance

The modernist city is built on a sense of mechanical order and efficiency. Yet harmony, a harmonious arrangement of our human environment, implies more than order. Part of the aesthetics of a healthy city, which contrasts with the need for purely efficient mechanics, is the way it facilitates the transcendence of static order. The kinds of space theories that planners impose on city environments in order to 'make sense' of them are frequently totalitarian. In his essay 'Walking in the City',[18] Michel de Certeau expressed one of his favourite themes, that of 'resistance' to systems that leave no room for otherness and transgression. The 'weak' – in this case, those who actually live in the city, rather than stand to one side and merely plan it – find ways to make space for themselves and to express their self-determination. What de Certeau calls 'the urbanistic system' attempts to define a 'literal meaning' of geometrical space that is similar to 'proper meanings' in language – as constructed by grammarians rather than by usage.

De Certeau writes of the almost erotic pleasure and temptation of 'seeing the whole', of looking down on the city and thereby totalizing it. He uses the image of standing at the top of the World Trade Center – a particularly potent yet painful choice of images since September 11, 2001. There we are (or were) able to be lifted out of Manhattan's grasp – we become voyeurs, not walkers. We can then 'read' the city as a text. But this is really an illusion. As de Certeau puts it: 'The fiction of this kind of knowledge is related to a lust to be a viewpoint, and nothing more.'[19] De Certeau compares this way of seeing to the aloofness of the urban planner or theorist. Meanwhile, the ordinary practitioners of the city live 'down below'. For de Certeau, what he called the 'Concept-city' of modernist abstraction was decaying. What outlives this decay is 'the microbe-like, singular and plural practices which an urbanistic system was supposed to control or suppress'.[20] These practices are what make the city lived space, as opposed to mere concept space. Such urban practices are plural and defy differentiation, classification and the imposition of social divisions and hierarchies.

Those who 'practise' the city are the people who actually walk its streets. This dimension of the city is what de Certeau called the 'noise' – the 'difference', the 'otherness', that is a city's life blood, without which it will die or become an empty shell. That is why, in de Certeau's aesthetic of a city, the role of indeterminacy is so important. He refers to this in terms of 'casual time': 'Thus, to eliminate the unforeseen or expel it from calculations as an illegitimate accident and an obstacle to rationality is to interdict the possibility of a living and "mythical" practice of the city.'[21]

De Certeau placed a strong emphasis on the power of narrative to shape human environments and transform them. Indeed, in terms of everyday life in the city, it is human narrative, as much as architecture or urban planning, that shapes identity and enables people to *use* the city as a means of creative or effective living:

> In modern Athens, the vehicles of mass transportation are called *metaphorai*. To go to work or come home, one takes a 'metaphor' – a bus or a train. Stories could also take this noble name: every day, they traverse and organize places; they select and link them together; they make sentences and itineraries out of them. They are spatial trajectories.[22]

De Certeau also stressed the importance of narrative to the practical articulation of everyday actions. Stories are more than descriptions: they also take ownership of spaces, and are therefore culturally and socially creative. Because human stories define boundaries and create bridges between individuals, narrative is a vital factor in the creation of the city as community, rather than merely an agglomeration of buildings and spaces. The narrative structure of such communities enables people to shape the world that surrounds them, rather than be passively controlled by it; it also creates ways of mapping the city and thus moving around it effectively.[23]

## *The subversive power of children*

An important factor in the resistance to the homogenization of city culture is the space children are allowed to occupy. 'Today, talking about the space of children is, most of all, talking about its absence,' sadly commented Professor Franco LaCecia in his 1999 lecture 'The space of play' at the Royal Society of Arts.[24] The place of children is one of the most potent indicators of how, in reality, the city is conceived and practised.[25] As a number of commentators have noted, the history of the modern city over the past 50 years has involved the progressive abandonment of most of the spaces that were once available to children for bodily movement. Arguably, one of the largest factors has been the problem of safety. The concept, however, of 'safety' is largely the product of the move towards the development of single-function spaces, where every activity is assigned its place and every space is defined in terms of specific function. This means that city spaces are frequently not 'possessed', or walked, in human bodily terms at certain times (outside work hours), by certain categories of people (the 'vulnerable') or at all.

In contrast, children have always represented an apparently chaotic and unpredictable way of using urban space. But is this not merely 'play'? In Western, 'grown-up' cities, 'play', if it has any value at all, is increasingly one activity among many that needs to be confined to its own functional space, called, for example, a 'leisure centre' (but even modern leisure is closer to serious targeted work than it is to play). Such centres, interestingly, are usually situated away from the centre, on the periphery of town. In other words, 'play' is marginalized from the heart of cities as something that does not fit in terms of the dominant values of efficiency and safety. 'Play' has no discernible productivity, and does not easily find a place within a results-focused culture. It seems to be on those terms that some New York City schools abolished 'playtime'! The status and role of children, therefore, particularly their invisibility except as instruments in promoting consumer concepts (to quote one telling journalistic phrase, 'from person of the future to handbag of now'), is not merely a statement about cities, but about our concept of human personhood. This is reduced to rationality, efficiency and productivity. Certain kinds of non-productive people, including children, become a 'liability' and therefore a worry.

Perhaps reducing children to the stereotype of 'those who play' is itself a problem. 'Play' seems to be an adult category that neatly bypasses how seriously, and with what complexity, children experience and practise their inner and outer worlds. What adults describe as 'play' is, for children, 'a practice of everyday life'. In reality, children are among the most powerful challenges to the city as planned space. They automatically transgress boundaries and insist on promoting a multifunctional approach, in contrast to the adult preference for single-function spaces. Adults think about violence and traffic and children's safety (along with that of other so-called vulnerable or non-productive groups), yet miss the underlying question: what is a safe city? In the urban thinking of people like de Certeau and his pupil Augé, the truly human city is a place of embodiment, rather than a place defined by abstractions of the mind. In so many ways, children stand for an embodied, rather than purely mental, practice of life. In other words, the truly human city is where the human body, and the collective body of the citizenry, dominate; where the streets are still walked in ways that defy pure function, and non-planned space invites people to imagine creatively a multitude of human possibilities. 'Cities are safe only as long as streets are a place for human living: crowded, multifunctional, open to every kind of passing and staying. Only an inhabited street can avoid here the danger of an inhuman city.'[26]

## Recovering the city

Some people have suggested that we should turn our backs on the city in pursuit of a rural idyll. Apart, however, from the logistical impossibility of such a massive social reversal, the danger is that unless we solve problems of alienation at another level, we carry it with us to another place. We do not need to flee the city so much as to repossess it for all people, by day and by night. In fact, what we need to do is confront the fundamental question: 'Why cities – what are cities for?'[27] In our Western world, they no longer have a strictly practical role as a defence against attack or a refuge against wild beasts. Even the more recent rationale for cities during the past two hundred years – the city as focus for economic systems and the organization of production – is ceasing to be as necessary as it was. The decentralization of industry, and the as yet only half-realized impact of information-technology living, mean that the complexity of cities is less and less necessary for efficient work or for the distribution of goods. Information technology is also likely to confront the previously unquestioned role of the city as the centre for information and for education. I do not believe that this means the end of the city, or even the end of these traditional functions, but the beginning of a new phase.

In the future, the city is most likely to find its meaning within the wider requirements of human culture. There will have to be far greater reflection on the civilizing possibilities of the city, and the opportunities it may offer for community, or social humanization, and cultural meaning. This implies that the aesthetic and moral potential of cities will increasingly take over from economic or other functional purposes. Such potential includes a number of things that, in terms of immediacy, are difficult to pin down, but which are critical. Cities have a unique capacity to focus a range of physical, intellectual and creative energies. They create new sets of cultural relationships simply because cities bring into regular contact a uniquely diverse range of activities. Cities have an unparalleled ability to combine diversities of age, ethnicity and cultures. Because of their relatively large size *and* the diversity of their spaces, cities are able to balance community and anonymity. As human environments, cities, when they work effectively, have an ability perpetually to undermine the defensive human instinct for enclosed assumptions and foregone conclusions.

This points increasingly to a new, or rather revived and deepened, central question: 'What is a humane city?' Theologically speaking, if the human city is merely an unavoidable environment for transit to somewhere else, the eternal city of God, its purpose is merely pragmatic. A certain interpretation of Augustine's theology of history leaves us with the sense that the city does not describe anything essential about what it is to be human, and is no more than an ephemeral shell for nomadic pilgrimage. By contrast, in the humane city, people would not only dwell, but belong – that is to say, be joined in attachments of affection and fulfilment. The humane city would enable the necessary space for individual personality to be balanced with a healthy collectivity. It would enable human aspirations to be productive, rather than repressed or diminished into self-indulgence. It would enable a proper connection to the world of nature, such that 'environment' or 'ecology' would not be distanced or placed in opposition to, but be continuous with and integrated with, people and their buildings.

The virtue of postmodern approaches to cities by architects, city planners and anthropologists is that they seek to rediscover the importance of a sense of place to human identity, to affirm human difference, to build community, to reshape public space and to plan built environments in accordance with human proportion, rather than in terms of standardization and depersonalizing bulk. We need, however, to be careful. Such approaches can sometimes fail to engage with the structural sins of power dominance, or excessive economic differentiation. Without a more critical approach to the nature of community, it is very difficult to prevent the creation of new public space, cleaned-up city centres and a café culture that once again insulates relative affluence from a new kind of social and cultural deprivation. The absence of social analysis all too easily reconfirms new forms of exclusion.

What is demanded, if cities are to have a long-term and meaningful future, is a reversal of the trend for them to represent merely a necessary evil. Traditional justifications (work, commerce, information and education) are likely to become increasingly unnecessary, or avoidable for those who can afford it. A long-term future demands the replacement of perceptions such as alienation, isolation, crime, congestion and pollution by community, participation, human energy, aesthetics and joy. In his much-commended 1995 BBC Reith Lectures, the British architect Richard Rogers summarized the current situation:

> The city has been viewed as an arena for consumerism. Political and commercial expediency has shifted the emphasis of urban development from meeting the broad social needs of the community to meeting the circumscribed needs of individuals. The pursuit of this narrow objective has sapped the city of its vitality. The complexity of 'community' has been untangled and public life has been dissected into individual components.

Paradoxically, in this global age of rising democracy, cities are increasingly polarising society into segregated communities.[28]

Rogers pleaded for the recovery of the concept of 'open-minded' space, which he borrowed from political theory. This is multifunctional and makes moral and spiritual, as well as literal, space for a variety of uses by a variety of people, in which everyone becomes a participant. Rogers's urban theory is a kind of secularized version of traditional religious concepts of hospitality. This kind of space contrasts with the current dominance of 'single-minded' space, which has one function predetermined from outside the environment and its participants by designers and planners. Both spaces may be necessary in any given urban community. Single-minded space responds to a modern need for autonomy and efficiency. However, without open-minded space as well, there are no places that give the inhabitants something in common or bring together a plurality of people.

There is a growing sense that public space needs to be reclaimed for all citizens. Historically, urban culture has 'worked' only when it has been fundamentally participatory. This sense of democratic participation demands physical expression and, for this, an 'open-minded' public realm is indispensable. Open-minded is not merely a question of the size of public spaces, for it is noticeable that the great totalitarian regimes of the twentieth century, on left and right, adopted sheer vastness and a monumental style of public space to intimidate and control the individual citizen. Public space needs to be accessible physically as well as 'intellectually' and spiritually, in the sense that, in its design, it should address the questions of community, social living and inclusivity for all citizens.

## Spiritual issues

In his definition of the sustainable city of the future, it is interesting that Richard Rogers adopted seven principles that are spiritual as much as, or more than, purely architectural or functional. A city will need to be:

- just (fundamentally accessible to all and participative)
- beautiful (with an aesthetic that uplifts the spirit)
- creative (able to stimulate the full potential of all its citizens and able to respond easily to change)
- ecological (where landscape and human action are integrated rather than in competition)
- 'of easy contact' (where communication in all senses is facilitated and where public spaces are communitarian)
- polycentric (integrating neighbourhoods and maximizing proximity)
- and finally, diverse.[29]

You will notice that these spiritual principles for cities are person-centred rather than design-centred. In Europe, there is a growing preoccupation with definitions of society, the nature of citizenship, civic life and the common good. Interestingly, one of the most influential independent British think-tanks, Demos, has produced a regular series of documentation on these areas; for example, Charles Leadbeater's *Civic Spirit: The Big Idea for a New Political Era*.[30] In the quest for a sufficient principle to organize society, the key word these days is 'mutuality', based on six elements: articulation (the individuality of all members); understanding (recognition of diversity); reconciliation (here understood as 'soft reconciliation', i.e. as in reconciling competing claims); action (co-operative effective choices); belonging (trust, goodwill, shared identity); and learning (adaptation). It's interesting, however, that when someone like Leadbeater comes to the question of how to improve mutuality in a society that has lost touch with it, he includes among his five critical concepts the word 'renunciation'. By this, he means the renunciation of the absolute claims of individual choice in favour of social cohesion. Then there is a problem. Leadbeater admits: 'Persuading people to be self-denying is a delicate and time-consuming process. It requires us to value restraint as a virtue as much as choice – a counterintuitive view in consumer society'.[31] Although he, and others, write about mutuality in terms of ethics, in the end they are stuck with the fundamental principle of effectiveness. Society will 'work better' if we behave in this way and adopt these values.

It seems to me that to talk about the city and citizenship as spiritual issues means more than this. If we want motivation to move beyond usefulness or effectiveness (which is not to say these are not important), we clearly need to move in the direction of a more developed vision of 'the human spirit' and what promotes its enhancement. In Christian terms, ethics and spirituality these days clearly overlap to a great degree. They are not, however, absolutely indistinguishable. In the end, spirituality is directly concerned not just with values or commitments, but with our desire, with what we love most deeply – our desire fundamentally to respond to 'the holy' or 'the sacred'.

When it comes to the specific contribution of Christian spirituality to reflection about the humane city, we face something of a problem. Our faith lives and the religious institutions that have so long framed them were shaped, at least until recently, by a contrast between a raucous cityscape and a peaceful, contemplative 'elsewhere' – whether rural life, a retreat house or a monastery. In other words, contemplation has so often been viewed as something that requires freedom from the distractions of everyday concerns. So can spirituality, specifically Christian spirituality, offer urban dreams? Surely it must, because the city is a site for exploring our humanity and that, spiritually speaking, lies at the heart of our spiritual sensibilities.

So the first thing to say is that a spirituality of urban living necessarily engages with 'the practice of everyday life'. The question is: 'How is this practice a contemplative experience?' One 'solution' might be a modern version of Augustine's *vita mixta* (the mixed life) – a rhythm of loving service of others in everyday life interspersed with, and balanced by, withdrawal from this work into the quiet of prayer. However, it is still the case that this 'withdrawal' is conceived as a privileged moment for engaging with the mystical foretaste of ultimate union with God. No, what we need is to re-read the contemplative tradition such that contemplative union may occur precisely in and through engagement with the everyday.

Mystical union can then be understood as a participation in the life of a God who is present and active *within* history, rather than detached or removed from it. It is then, in joining ourselves to this work, that we find God in all things.

Of course, this does not imply that simply doing our every-day tasks – any action at all – is automatically a context for a mysticism of the everyday. God's saving work in history is, for example, an action of transformation, of hospitality for all, of the reconciliation of all things and peoples. Similarly, a mystical participation in God's work in history demands a pro-phetic, culturally and socially critical engagement – not just a placid acceptance of immediate things as they are.

I want to end with one deeply serious spiritual issue: the nature of reconciliation. In Christian terms, human commun-ity involves reconciliation – in this case, 'hard reconciliation'. While there are some quite negative biblical images of the city, for example in Genesis, where Cain the murderer becomes the first city-dweller, there is another biblical image in the Jerusa-lem tradition, for example in the psalms. Here the city also expresses the peace of God. Those who live in the city are required to share God's peace with one another. 'Hence the city is called to realize a justice that is more than giving each person his due: it is to give God his due, by building the city that his peace, presence and forgiveness make possible, so that all his people may share it together.'[32]

From a Christian standpoint, people are created in the image of a Trinitarian God. Trinitarian faith has a particular

87

capacity to hold unity and multiplicity together. This offers a way beyond the contemporary tendency (reflected in much postmodern writing) for community, and indeed the individual 'self', to fragment into a 'pastiche of personalities'. The Christian revelation of God suggests a dialectical relationship between what is unique and particular, and what is universal, or between what is personal and what is interdependent. Trinitarian belief affirms God as a space in which the particularity of the divine persons is not merely held in tension with, but consists of, their interrelatedness and communion. The portrayal of God as persons-in-communion can be translated into an image of human well-being as 'personal space' that is indistinguishably 'space for the other'.

For Christians, this catholicity or inclusivity of God is expressed sacramentally most explicitly in the 'communion' of believers, shaped by the spirit of the Risen Jesus in the practice of the Eucharist. The Eucharist is not simply a matter of piety, but is the enactment of the identity of the Christian community in and for the world. This enactment of identity opens the believing community to ways of living in and for the world, in and for the city, as a catalyst of reconciliation. Every celebration of the Eucharist in the city marks out, if you like, an ethical space in the midst of what is existentially a flawed and ambiguous reality. To quote from the 1982 World Council of Churches document on the Eucharist:

> The Eucharist embraces all aspects of life . . . The Eucharistic celebration demands reconciliation and sharing among all those regarded as brothers and sisters in the one family of God and is a constant challenge in the search for appropriate relationships in social, economic and political life . . . All kinds of injustice, racism, separation and lack of freedom are radically challenged when we share in the body and blood of Christ . . . As participants in the Eucharist, therefore, we prove inconsistent if we are not actively participating in this ongoing restoration of the world's situation and the human condition.[33]

At the heart of the Eucharist is the critical theme of reconciliation. This goes far deeper than mere tolerance. Interestingly, the *Oxford English Dictionary* refers not merely to the restoration of harmony, but to the 'reconsecration of desecrated places'. If you like, all those whose lives and identities are marginalized and disempowered in the human city are 'desecrated places' whose unique worth as images of God is denied. Reconciliation, therefore, demands repentance by all of us whose attitudes and actions promote the exclusion or diminishment of 'the other'. Only when there is substantial repentance can there also be effective forgiveness. There needs, too, to be a commitment to refuse to participate in structures or behaviours that violate the other in whatever way. In positive terms, there is always restitution after repentance. Restitution is not necessarily or solely economic but includes such things as restoring the value or identity of the other, or enabling the empowerment of others. Because restitution involves the establishment of a just situation, this will always entail loss for some so that others may gain. Restitution is also bound up with reconstruction – the reconstruction of a quite different world of discourse and practice.

The city as a place of reconciliation in this sense is not a melting pot in which diverse cultures are invited to submerge their differences into a new homogeneous identity. The city, as place of reconciliation, is a space for socially, racially, culturally and religiously diverse voices to find their unique place to speak and to be heard. A Christian understanding of reconciliation suggests that it is precisely in making room for what is unlike that each and every person is enabled to become different and, together, to become more than anyone could be in isolation.

# 7

## *Urban spirituality: one size does not fit all*

### Bernadette Flanagan

———◆◆◆———

Adapting a famous statement by Stephen Bevans, a professor of mission theology, it is my belief that there is no such thing as spirituality; there is only contextual spirituality.[1] Bevans has developed six snapshots of the way Christians go about exploring the presence of God in the various contexts in which they find themselves: Translation, Anthropological, Praxis, Synthetic, Transcendental and Countercultural. The models Bevans has developed can be of assistance, I believe, in understanding the diversity that exists in approaches to seeking the presence of God in the city today – that is, urban spirituality.

### *Translation models*

The translation approach to spirituality claims that the message of the Scriptures is unchanging, but it struggles to liberate that message from historical limitations of time or place, and to translate the meaning of Scripture and tradition into a new setting. This is an approach to urban spirituality evident in the writings emanating from the Paris-based Jerusalem communities. The mission of the monastic Communities of Jerusalem, founded in Saint Gervais Church, Paris, on All Saints' Day 1975 by Fr. Pierre-Marie Delfieux, in collaboration with Cardinal François Marty, is to 'work in the city, pray in the city, work and pray for the city, weep and sing with the city'.[2]

Their life has five distinctive characteristics. In response to the phenomenon of urbanization, they have chosen to be city-dwellers. Their horarium is set by the rhythm of the comings and goings of the working population in the city. They are committed to being wage-earners as an act of solidarity with the city's mass of workers, regardless of whether or not their work corresponds to their professional training. They have chosen not to protect their monastic way of life by the enclosure of walls, but seek instead to stay focused in their hearts. Their fifth option is to be part of the diocesan church, in the spirit of Vatican II, in order to live fully the reality of the local church, and to better adapt to different situations and cultures.

Their Rule of Life begins its reflection on the call to give expression to a living faith in the city with a quotation from the Acts of the Apostles: 'Get up, go into the city and you will be told what to do' (Acts 9.6). It does not situate its hope in God's presence in the city in any social or religious movement, but in the multiple scriptural references to God's action in the city.[3] It proceeds by establishing a correspondence between the situation of biblical cities and the modern city. The inclusion of 'Jerusalem' within the title chosen for the community clearly reflects the translation dynamic of the community's spirituality.

A second inspiration clearly evident in the Rule of Life of the Jerusalem community is that of the desert mothers and fathers. In using these resources, the community views the city as a contemporary desert and imagines the possible reversal of the spiritual movement from city to desert, which third-century Christians initiated. This is because city and desert have now swapped the significance they had in those times. What defined a city in ancient times was its walls.[4] The very word 'city' (*ir*) in Hebrew means 'an enclosed place'. Under attack, people fled their fields and villages and headed for the nearest city. The desert, on the other hand, was a place without walls, a place where demons roamed, a lonely place. To live in the desert was to live undefended, to expose oneself to the elements and sleep lightly. Today, in the vision of the Jerusalem communities, the city's walls have fallen. It is no longer a place to go to be safe, but a place to go to be challenged, to wrestle with the modern-day demons of crime and consumerism, of homelessness and violence.[5]

While Saint-Gervais is one of the best-known expressions of contemporary urban monastic spirituality, there are many other expressions, such as Our Lady of the City Hermitage in Spokane, Washington state.[6] Cecilia W. Wilms, hermit of Our Lady of the City Hermitage, who died there on 13 May 1998, discovered a solitary way to 'live my monastic commitment in the desert of the city in the service of God and the Church'. As Catholic Church law did not provide at this time for a public commitment to the hermit way of living, Cecilia received the Consecration of Virgins through the ministry of Bishop Bernard Topel of Spokane in 1974.

Not all forms of urban monasticism, however, are communal. The eremitical strand is also well represented, as, for example, is the case in the life of Hugette, who left the Carmelite cloister for a Brussels attic.[7] Like the Jerusalem community, her way of life was deeply inspired by the life of the third-century desert hermits, as the anonymity that their desert hermitages provided was equally available to her in the immensity of the modern city.

In their use of Scripture and tradition, the spirituality of the Jerusalem community and of other new urban monastic centres exhibits a translation approach to the challenge of urbanization. The basic principle is to take the focus on the city, which echoes through Christian history, and to reincarnate it in one of today's great urban settings. They seek to make present in the city, in a quiet and unobtrusive way, the abiding concern of God for the chosen city of Jerusalem.

## *Praxis models*

In the praxis model, God's urban presence is primarily discerned not through God's word about the city, but in the historical fabric of life in the city, particularly in the stories of those who minister to oppressed urban peoples struggling for liberation. This model of spirituality nourishes a continual dialogue between the heritage of faith and the experience of hearing the voice of God in the struggle of marginalized city-dwellers.

While urban monasticism uses the biblical significance of the city as its starting point for urban spirituality, the praxis model privileges solidarity with the experience of poor city-dwellers who seek to be attentive to God in the city. The presupposition of this model is that the Scriptures reveal God's desire for all to experience the fullness of life. There is, therefore, a need for committed Christians to be attentive to, and to challenge, structures that thwart the realization of this desire of God for all humanity, especially city-dwellers. One typical manifestation of this type of urban spirituality is the Sojourners community. The Sojourners[8] community and magazine were founded in Chicago in 1971, by evangelical seminary students. Inspired by the text of Hebrews 11, which speaks of the People of God as exiles on earth, the name 'Sojourners' expresses the distance that the community has felt between itself and American society, but also reflects a desire to get involved in building a Christian community at a local level.

Jim Wallis, editor of *Sojourners* magazine, has pointed out that the origins of their expression of spirituality in the city lay in wrestling with the gospel call to radical discipleship. In fact, they began their days together as a community by studying every verse in the Bible that talked about God's love for the poor. They were struck by the fact that, in the Hebrew Bible, the suffering of the poor was the second most prominent theme, idolatry being the first – though the two were often connected. In the New Testament, they found that one out of every 16 verses was about the poor. Through their study, they concluded that 'the oldest and best traditions of the Church demand that the gospel be proclaimed and lived in the midst of the suffering world, and that those who follow Jesus Christ be particularly sensitive to the poor and oppressed'.[9] The community has, since its inception, sought to give expression to these insights in the context of the inner city. They chose to live in Columbia Heights, a poor black neighbourhood just east of the White House. Their ministry there involved a tenant organization, a food-distribution programme, support groups for parents and programmes for children. In their Sunday Eucharist, these involvements were challenged through reflection on, and sharing in the community, the Scripture readings for the day.

The spirituality of those who belong to the Sojourners community is well expressed in a reflection by one of its members in its newsletter:

> I live in the city to be a witness against violence and injustice, and to experience first-hand its human and structural dynamics. As a result, diminished dignity and the pressures of poverty are not merely concepts to me. When I stand in long lines at the few grocery stores, where prices are higher than in the suburbs and the food is of lower quality, I understand demoralization; when I allow encounters with human tragedy to become part of my prayer life, rather than denying they exist, I understand the paradox of faith as my trust in God deepens.[10]

At the heart of this model is reflective action. The praxis approach is not, however, a simple focusing on 'doing the truth'. Rather, it is committed to overcoming the gap between reflection and action, and so attempts to become more engaged in both activities.

## Synthetic models

Bevans has described the synthetic approach as a middle-of-the-road model – midway between personal reflective immersion in the *present* existential reality of the city (praxis model), and appreciative appropriation of the *past* biblical urban vision (translation model).[11] The praxis model seeks to generate a communal dialogue between the Word of God, rigorous sociocultural analyses of the city and the lived experience of city-dwellers.

The ripeness for such a development in urban spirituality was recognized by the Church of England after 30 cities in England erupted in street violence in 1981.[12] The Passionist priest Austin Smith, who spent a lifetime in city ministry and is the author of *Passion for the Inner City*,[13] articulated the insight that was dawning:

> The Inner City is more than the Inner City. Though it may be a physical reality, it is also a frightening symbol in our land and becomes so increasingly. It is the symbol of the ever-increasing divide between the powerful and the powerless, the hopeful and the hopeless, the able and the disabled.[14]

Clergy and bishops in the centres of the riots fed a continuous stream of reports into the office of Archbishop Robert Runcie. He took the initiative of establishing an independent commission to report to him directly. The commission was established in 1983 with the following terms of reference:

> To examine the strengths, insights, problems and needs of the Church's life and mission in Urban Priority Areas and, as a result, to reflect on the challenge which God may be making to Church and Nation: and to make recommendations to appropriate bodies.[15]

The commission, which was made up of a heterogeneous group of 18 people, worked together between July 1983 and

September 1985 and produced a unanimous report. It was, for the whole group, a spiritual experience:

> . . . somewhere along the road we have travelled in the past two years each of us has faced a personal challenge to our lives and lifestyles: a call to change our thinking and action in such a way as to help us to stand more closely alongside the risen Christ with those who are poor and powerless. We have found faith in the city.[16]

In the nearly 20 years since the publication of *Faith in the City*, many of the problems faced by inner-city and outer-estate communities have failed to disappear; but the fact that for the twentieth anniversary of *Faith in the City* the Commission on Urban Life and Faith has been established to report on the new contexts and challenges that exist in towns and cities in the United Kingdom bears witness to the cry of the city receiving attentive listening. Central to this practice of corporate urban spiritual accompaniment is the development of theological reflection and dialogue on urban life and faith: achieving a better understanding of the processes and policies shaping life in urban communities, promoting dialogue with city-life decision-makers and a commitment to the mode of reflective practitioner by those who minister in the city.

One common feature of the three approaches above is that spirituality in the city is, for the most part, viewed from the outside, from the insights of those ministering in city communities, rather than from inside the experience of the regular city-dweller. From an anthropological point of view, the above approaches are etic (that is, they are informed by the desire to interpret local people's doing, thinking, feeling according to the researcher's predetermined categories), rather than emic (which is the desire to know what local people see themselves doing, thinking, feeling). What would happen if there was a revaluing of the experience of long-term city-dwellers, and if this experience was actively engaged in the shaping of ritual, spirituality, services, ministry? In particular, would this require a re-evaluation of the symbols of Christian worship, symbols such as Jesus the shepherd, which draws on a rural agricultural context unfamiliar to urban technological experience? The next two models give primacy of attention to the everyday experience of the city-dweller in outlining a vision of urban spirituality.

## Anthropological models

Those who employ the anthropological model, while taking the Bible, sociological analysis and the experience of those who serve in the city seriously, also seek God's self-revelation within the intrinsic values, relational patterns, environment, rhythms and concerns of ordinary city-dwellers. The focus of spiritual accompaniment for those who operate within the parameters of this model is to attend to the trace of God's presence in the landscape of the city. Its guiding conviction is that God has not been hidden from any people at any time, or in any place, but rather accompanies them, by day and by night. By applying the techniques of ethnography, the practitioner of this model attempts to attend to the search for meaning within the complex structures of urban life. This vision of urban spirituality implicitly has inspired Colin Marchant's *Signs in the City*[17] and Gill Goulding's *On the Edge of Mystery*.[18]

The spiritualities in this model are characterized by their immersion in the physical realities of the city. Colin Marchant, a Baptist minister, has spent a lifetime ministering in East London. He has aligned his work with that of the prophet Jeremiah,[19] particularly the latter's efforts to identify 'signs of stress' and 'signs of hope' for his own people. The signs of stress in the street are 'deep-rooted, widespread and growing in intensity', he believes.[20] For those who have eyes to see, these signs appear in the most unexpected places. Informed by Marchant's prophetic approach, I have taken a closer look at Christmas trees in the inner-city quarters of Dublin. This has revealed, for example, that some are covered with floral, rather than holly, wreaths. These trees are being used in the annual family festival to commemorate the memory of all those brothers, sisters, mothers, fathers, sons and daughters who had died as a result of drugs in the year coming to an end. This is a warning sign for the future. The message is clear: the children of God in the inner city want to make known their despair and grief; they feel powerless and invite those passing to cross the road, in the tradition of the Good Samaritan, and ask them how they might respond with compassion to the pain in the city.

When the city is viewed from the perspective of signs of hope,[21] Marchant focuses in particular on the clustering of individuals and groups in the city to address the situation in which they find themselves.[22] The energetic and transformative spirituality emerging from this movement is also witnessed in Gill Goulding's analysis of the Hope Community in Wolverhampton. The new style of Christian community is one where residents in a flat complex build a network of supportive relationships rooted in the everyday realities of urban life. The Hope Community was founded in the Heath Town estate in Wolverhampton in 1984.[23] It has a nucleus of Infant Jesus religious sisters, an inner circle of temporarily committed resident members and a wider circle of neighbours and friends. The community seeks to provide a place where the sense of God's presence in the experience of life will be intentionally cultivated and celebrated. A fundamental practice in the community for nourishing hope in the lives of those who dwell on the urban margins is the practice of contemplative listening, the exercise of a spiritual hermeneutic of words that 'may well be most ordinary and commonplace'.[24]

The goal of many community services in the city may be to remove some impediments to the well-being of the city-dweller, or to solve some problem. Once the impediment has been removed, or the problem solved, the helping relationship ends. In the anthropological approach to urban community-building, however, the goal is to continually deepen the experience of what it means to be a human being who lives on the urban margins, amid the traffic, buildings, crowds and multiculturalism that characterize city life. The faith of the members of these communities directly seeks to engage the configuration of the city in the way they organize for worship.

The second expression of the anthropological approach to urban spirituality exists in the work of the Urban Theology Unit in Sheffield, founded in 1969. It is an independent ecumenical educational charity, founded by John Vincent, a Methodist minister. His reflection on his work as director of an urban theology centre locates his starting point in the 'hermeneutical privilege of the urban poor'.[25] There is, he believes, a new readiness in the dweller on the urban margins to hear the gospel. In particular, he identifies three experiences of poor city-dwellers that find a resonance in the gospel. To these people, it is remarkable that Jesus belonged to the common people and experienced the frustration that resulted from having intolerable economic, political and religious oppression brought to bear on them. In this frustration, Jesus assumed a confrontational stance. So, the city-dweller feels their anger validated and their protests supported. Jesus did not, however, protest alone. His was a movement carried forward by disciples. Thus, the kinship bonds that characterize inner-city life are given a new significance. In these are the seeds of a new flowering of gospel community in the city, John Vincent believes.

Central to the anthropological model of urban spirituality is the belief that one of the most radical disadvantages suffered by the powerless and the marginalized in society is their exclusion from conversations that create society. Those who espouse this model are therefore seeking to find ways to address this exclusion. Their aim is to find structures and practices that will help the voice of the voiceless and the power of the powerless to truly become a part of the voice and strength of the churches, rather than the churches creating a ministry to the city among their other involvements.

## *Transcendental models*

Assuming that the human mind operates in similar ways in all cultures, the transcendental approach to urban spirituality is concerned with the struggle for authenticity of a particular subject, conditioned by history, geography and culture.[26] Thus, the personal journey of the city-dweller has a greater priority in this model than the communal journey, which is privileged in the anthropological model above. This approach to spirituality has its foundations in theologies such as those of Karl Rahner and Bernard Lonergan.[27] Although this might, at first glance, appear to be a very personal and individualistic starting point, this is not necessarily negative, as the encounter with dwelling on the urban margins is uniquely appropriated by each person. What would seem like a narrow starting point may actually be the best starting point for exploring the contours of a spirituality that builds bridges across communities, rather than further isolating the city-dweller, as it is located in an exploration of the common hopes and joys, fears and anxieties of the human person.

In my work *The Spirit of the City: Voices from Dublin's Liberties*,[28] I sought, using this approach to urban spirituality, to bring to the surface the expressions of five forms of postmodern spirituality among city-dwellers in Dublin. From the outset, I wanted to establish that the relationship between cultural change and religious expression is complex, multidimensional and translocational. I found, however, that the evidence seemed to indicate that conditions of life in the city did influence the particular expression of any generic form of postmodern spirituality. My data was drawn from extended interviews with the long-term residents of a historic quarter in Dublin's inner city, the Liberties. I found, for example, that among those interviewed, the postmodern turn to apophatic[29] expressions of spirituality arose most strongly among those whose lives were being cut short by HIV infection and drug addiction. One person whose apophatic spirituality was supported by the 12-step addiction-recovery plan succinctly expressed her belief in God's power in her life, in the face of a profound sense of God's absence, in the aphorism: 'You've got to fake it to make it'.

The stress in the data of the interviews fell most strongly on resisting a grand spiritual vision that could alienate people from the everyday reality of life's experience in Dublin's inner city. An illustration of this trend was evident in the following contribution:[30]

'Your reward will be great in Heaven' [Luke 6.23]: that was a phrase that I grew up with. And I hate that, because I don't want my reward to be great in Heaven. You know I want some kind of decent life now. So my hope is not for something fantastically brilliant, but hope that in struggling, whatever you're struggling for, you know, to keep your family together, for food on the table, to make a difference at community level, whatever; that in all that struggle you're making a difference, the fact that you continue to struggle, to not give up, to not say 'nothing is possible'. I suppose it's very difficult to sustain a sense of people's decency sometimes, yes? Because crime is a huge feature of life here and violence is a huge feature of life here, you know? And so hope has something to do with seeing beneath that, you know? And believing like we're more than that or we can be more than that. Does that make sense? Just belief that chaos won't win and that through small actions you make a difference.

The findings of these interviews called out to be carried forward, I believed, in the establishment of listening spaces in the city. In these settings, skilled listeners would seek to uncover some of the images and happenings that keep those who live in the city awake, pondering: what do they mean? Among the resources that could enable those in the city to give expression to questions within their soul, the arts must be particularly privileged. So often, urban aesthetics, especially in poor communities, can quench the spirit. Urban centres of soul-listening could challenge this aesthetic famine that stalks the lives of inner-city dwellers by providing introductions to dance, music and colour as privileged languages of communication for expressing the urban soul struggle. So often, access to the arts has been the prerogative of a cultural elite. Beauty has the same power to speak to the soul of the city-dweller as it has to any other person, so the establishment of locations in the city that open up access to the beautiful requires urgent attention.

In this model, then, an urban spirituality can be generated only by a dialogue with the lived experience of the urbanite. As in every dialogue, the outcome cannot be predicted. From the conversation, both the interviewer and the interviewee will go away with questions. As a result, the gospel is broken open in new ways and in a new setting. This model places a high value on hearing about the efforts of the ordinary person, in any context, to struggle with belief. With its focus on attending to the religious journey, rather than the religious destination, of the individual urbanite, this approach to urban spirituality is distinctly heuristic in its method of inquiry.

## *Countercultural models*

> . . . cities and battered women have been 'mythed upon'. They have been named 'whore of Babylon' or 'Bride of New Jerusalem' . . . Cities, like battered women, suffer from a dualistic myth. As long as they are first named 'virgin bride', they will soon be victimized as 'battered whore'.[31]

The above reflection by Letty Russell alerts us to a darker reading of the city that also exists in theological circles. Unlike the previous five models of spirituality, which search for God in urban experience, the countercultural model warns of the possible extinguishing of the God spark in the city.

In this countercultural approach to spirituality, the prima facie assumption that life in the city is the ground for religious experience does not operate. In sympathy with the work of postliberal theologians like George Lindbeck, this approach to spirituality contends that contemporary Christians ought not begin with their experience today, then try to make the Bible and faith beliefs fit into it; instead, they must be able to let the Bible's language and narratives make sense of their lives in biblical terms. Rudolf Siebert has referred to this as a 'negative political theology', because it stresses what must be overcome in a contemporary social situation, such as the city, in order to realize the Kingdom. Postliberals have been consistently critical of most forms of expression of Christian concern by the Churches, and argue for a radical discontinuity between Christianity and any given culture or context.

The postliberal theologian Stanley Hauerwas has argued that churches should be contrast models to sociocultural patterns, 'a political alternative to every nation'.[32] His argument is that theology and spirituality since the Enlightenment have tended to ask the wrong question: how to make the gospel credible in the modern (urban) world? Instead, he asserts that the Christian faith is an invitation to be part of what he terms an 'alien people'.[33] There is a constant call echoing through postliberal writings for the Church to renew itself as a distinctive community. He is also unhappy that Christian politics has come to mean Christian social activism:

> Much of what passes for Christian social concern today, of the left or right, is the social concern of a Church that seems to have despaired of being Church.[34]

The challenge for the Church in the present cultural climate is, in the countercultural view, the formation of a faithful community that, through faith and vision, grows into being a countercultural social structure. In a postliberal, countercultural approach to urban spirituality, the city would be more strongly identified with being a place of darkness.[35] This countercultural emphasis is evident in the writings of John Paul II, who also highlights the fact that the city can be the home for those who have nowhere else to go, a place of exile, uprootedness and displacement.[36]

> The fact is that many people, perhaps the majority today, do not have the means which would enable them to take their place in an effective and humanly dignified way. Allured by the dazzle of an opulence which is beyond their reach, and at the same time driven by necessity, these people crowd the cities of the Third World, where they are often without cultural roots, and where they are exposed to situations of violent uncertainty, without the possibility of becoming integrated. Their dignity is not acknowledged in any real way, and sometimes there are even attempts to eliminate them from history through coercive forms of demographic control which are contrary to human dignity.

He also portrays the city as a scene fraught with inequality, violence and addiction.[37] Thus, the biblical reflection on the city as the archetypal representation of the erring, unfaithful disciple, referred to by Letty Russell, is translated into a modern context. All is not well in the city, and the task of decrying the dehumanization wrought on many persons by urban attention may be as pressing a challenge for the contemporary minister as the call to assert that God dwells within the city.

In conclusion, then, it is evident that several different approaches exist in the practice of finding God in the city today. This pluralism is not something that will go away. Rather than this analysis acting as a map on which each reader tries to locate his or her style, preference or conviction regarding urban spirituality, the hope is that it will invite reflection on the paths to God not yet discovered in the urban landscape.

# 8

## *The spirituality of everyday life*

### Andrew Davey

To write about 'urban spirituality' is to launch oneself into numerous debates about definition and experience. The shape and nature of urban life is receiving great attention across the disciplines at a moment when, for the first time in human history, the majority of the world's population lives in cities. While there is some disagreement about the exact definition of a 'city' – in terms of population levels, densities and governance – urban life is a lived reality through the experience of propinquity, the negotiation of diversity, the concrete reality of the built environment and the noise, speed and pollution of contemporary metropolitan attention.

'Spirituality', meanwhile, attracts a great deal of attention and debate, from the burgeoning Mind, Body, Spirit shelves of large (urban) bookshops to the proliferation of (usually non-urban) locations of spiritual depth. Yet the range of calls on spirituality, not least this growing tendency to turn it into some kind of commodity, may suggest that we need to treat it with a certain amount of caution. Stephen Sykes has recently written of the danger of associating spirituality merely with ideas of well-being and with making sense of life, while denying the need to establish a 'God-centred account' of human experience.[1]

What is so different about prayer/spirituality in the city? How does the urban context affect the way we pray; and, in turn, how might our prayer affect the environment in which we pray? What are the strategies and tactics we might adopt? Urban settings have not always been seen as a conducive setting for 'things of the spirit'. The harsh anarchy of the industrial or commercial city has often been contrasted with the ordered serenity of the village green or cathedral close. Corruption is apparent in the smells, noise, pollution and the visual temptations. Hardly a place to pray; rather a place from which one could cry for release. The things of the spirit have usually stood in opposition to things of the flesh, but the breath, soul and enlivening of the spirit have usually been experienced in human community, and through very solid forms of art and architecture. The psalmist sings of a direct correlation between the pursuit of communal justice and the built environment.[2] God has loved the city, as a prototype of the final deliverance. The vision of the heavenly city stands firm against the pagan Elysian fields – a vast habitation where one can only wonder at its extent and inclusivity. The call to enter the new Jerusalem is one to participate in its maintenance, and to practise human freedom in the presence of God. The pursuit of the life of the spirit in the city reconnects us with that creative, communalizing vision and energy; it enables us to celebrate, and engage with, the life of the city in our quest for the 'new ordering of God' on earth as it is in heaven.

Location is vital. The places where we live, work, worship and encounter others are an essential part of the formation of our spirituality and theology. The practice of Christians in urban areas must be informed by what Roman Catholic documents call 'the integrating principle', in which there is an organic reality to the practice of faith and the pursuit of the kingdom's justice.[3] The practice of urban spirituality connects with what has been called 'doing local theology'; believing combines with practice, reflection with worship and prayer with everyday life. People learn what it means to be 'mindful of God' in their particular situation, to be attentive to the action of God in the world around them, to be ready to see their location with new eyes and to encounter the divine in its places and people. The individuality and privatization of what often passes for spirituality buys into a culture where one no longer trips over God on the pavement or in the doorway of the city church; instead, the city is seen as something to be escaped rather than revelled in.

In many ways, we have lost our ability to comprehend the spirituality that exists in the urban environment around us. The secularization of our cityscapes means that we rarely encounter the transcendent through built form or public art. Our medieval counterparts, however, would have been at home in a spiritual space where not just sacred buildings, but the sacredness of the built environment and of the community that occupied it, were taken for granted. Moving in a spiritual landscape was a significant aspect of the experience of pilgrimage, both during the actual journey and in the multisensory encounter at the, usually, urban destination, with its shrines and merchandising; spiritual disciplines were often laid out as part of the urban topography and of the 'living stones' who still inhabited the sacred places.[4] When travelling, cities were refuges, places of safety and sanctuary surrounded by the danger and instability of the countryside.

'Living stones' are the key to this: too often, we think of the city solely in terms of its buildings. At times, this may be the first impression: one only has to walk through the City of London on a weekend. But it is in the human city – the city of flesh and blood – that our struggles for spirituality must take place. We must reject the notion that the built environment has any power over individual or social forms. An urban spirituality must reinvest the city with the possibility of the sacred. This may involve participation in communal and public struggles to establish community – one that negotiates various forms of spiritual meaning and identity – as we encounter communities seeking their right to the city. These may be new immigrant groups seeking to establish space for worship, or minorities pursuing new identity and cultural agendas. In her visionary book *Towards Cosmopolis*, the Australian urbanist

Leonie Sandercock writes of the need to 'resacralize' urban space through new alliances that defy the imposition of 'dumb featureless public space . . . devoid of the spirit'.[5] Sandercock develops the notion of 'cosmopolis' – a city where people live with, make room for and celebrate difference by recognizing the contribution of each other's culture and spirituality. Cosmopolis is a utopian vision, 'a construction site of the mind' that can be glimpsed in numerous communal projects and acts of inclusion. Parallels with recent theological writing on the vision of God's kingdom come to mind.[6]

Cities are places of possibility and encounter. A stunning array of opportunities for personal and communal exploration presents itself to deep-rooted residents as well as to more recent arrivals. Old communal patterns change quickly, particularly in cities with many global connections. Away from the restraints of family and familiars, new identities become feasible. Fresh challenges and questions confront the seeker. Much has been written on the city as the place where encounters with the strange, and the stranger, are commonplace; in an urban neighbourhood, one can operate only in space that is always that of the other.[7] I believe that the seeds of any serious urban spirituality lie in this experience. Commenting on Charles Baudelaire, Richard Sennett says: 'The modern city can turn people outward, not inward; rather than wholeness the city can give them experiences of otherness. The power of the city to reorient people in this way lies in its diversity; in the presence of difference people have at least the opportunity to step outside themselves.'[8]

In urban communities, the huge differences in wealth and social access might give one the impression that spirituality is a luxury for the cultured and leisured classes. A spirituality that retains struggle and engagement can, however, bring new dimensions into the spiritual life of all communities in the city. The French urbanist Henri Lefebvre writes of the 'right to the city'[9] – the ability to connect with, and enjoy, the potentials and opportunities that urban culture offers. Through engaging with the life of the city, either explicitly or implicitly, the Christian community makes spaces for the spirit and enacts the life of the spirit within that cultural setting. While we cannot expect a pre-Enlightenment Christendom to be mediated by our city, we must expect our urban spirituality to be part of the reinhabiting and occupation of space and of the unifying of human longing for a social order that is a foretaste of the kingdom. The cultural critic (and former Jesuit) Michel de Certeau wrote of the 'practice of everyday life' – the demonstration of a mesh of practices through which the city is constantly appropriated and reshaped by its inhabitants, as they become producers of new spatial and social relations. The ordinariness of many of these tactics, such as talking, reading, shopping and playing, means that they will go unnoticed; the changes they produce will be negligible. Other tactics are about survival, about opportunities seized and the small victories of the weak over the strong; these may become strategies for more significant change when combined with the aspirations and energy of others.[10]

A number of groups have sought to combine this energy, Sennett's 'power to reorient', with the need to pray in, and for, the city. The Retreat on the Street, pioneered by the Faith in Leeds group, or the Urban Theology Unit's Urban Pilgrimage in Sheffield are examples of local initiatives that have attempted to provide an opportunity for encounter and reflection on the streets of particular inner-city and estate communities. The relocation of religious communities to poor urban communities often combines the vocation to serve with the task of creating sacred space and events within those places, and this may, at times, be deliberately implicit. One thinks of households based on the heritage of Charles de Foucauld, where the hidden life of Nazareth is lived with great simplicity and respect for those with whom that neighbourhood is shared.

Given that de Foucauld's practice was shaped in the context of predominantly Muslim communities, he may be a more than appropriate model for Christian presence in the neighbourhoods of many European cities. In an age of globalization, the urban encounter with a stranger takes on new dimensions. Bishop Theodore Eastman wrote of how one can no longer separate 'those who are far off from those who are near'.[11] Unfamiliar spiritualities begin to map out new urban terrains; strangers become neighbours, and begin to negotiate a shared space of community. Leonie Sandercock writes of how often it is the city planning department that is the first to encounter these changes, as groups seek space for worship and congress. The new ethnicities of our cities will also be present within the Christian community, bringing with them new narratives, insights and practices. The potential for celebrating such heritage in diversity was apparent in a celebration of All Souls' Day that I attended at the Episcopalian Cathedral in Los Angeles; it brought together rites of the Mexican Day of the Dead with similar rites from the Korean community. One can think of other examples of new presences becoming apparent in urban liturgies, such as the singing of a Yoruba invocation at Pentecost, the offering of South Indian dance in a service of light or new insights into the use of the Bible from Filipino members. Within our urban church, we have a very real opportunity to reclaim the catholicity of our liturgy and spirituality.

Through the offering of the Eucharist, the offices, prayer and the sharing of Scriptures, Christians have a collection of tactics through which they can begin to reimagine and reshape the communities and context of which they are part. Liturgy in the city often becomes 'a counter-cultural activity . . . the means through which Christians stake their interest in a place by creating events, new histories – concrete, historicized acts that proclaim God's new order'.[12] Sacramental presence is lived: 'The Christ who now lives extends his living in the world through us.'[13] The Church of England, in its parish system, retains a spirituality of spatial awareness, of a sacred geography of embeddedness and engagement. Our church buildings are often the only permanences in rapidly shifting cityscapes, as local employment, institutions and associations are eroded. In many ways, they are reminiscent of the wells of earlier cities, which remained vital focuses for neighbourhoods and households through centuries of rebuilding. The sustainability of such a presence must be a vital concern for those considering the future life of the Church and its need to draw on appropriate models for spirituality and Christian discipleship across our predominantly urban society – and particularly in the marginalized and fragmented neighbourhoods that often exist alongside areas of wealth production and economic power.

Poor urban neighbourhoods, as well as suburban areas, might be included when Stephen Sykes comments, in his Anglican ecclesiology: 'Would it not be consistent with the Anglican tradition to see our churches offering praise on behalf of a specific part of the world which God loves, the praise which it has forgotten to express?'[14] In realizing an urban spirituality, those strategies come together as the Christian community becomes more aware of a memory that heals, redeems and transforms, of a narrative that, when told and prayed in community, allows the integrating principle to take root. In his Dimbleby Lecture, the Archbishop of Canterbury saw the locatedness of the Church as essential to its ability to make a difference in the poorest communities, and in a culture disdainful of commitment to such a conviction:

> The sheer presence of the church – or any place of religious activity, in the middle of communities of primary deprivation such as I have been speaking about – indicates that there is still a space where you can give voice to these accounts of humanity. [The Church] is obliged just to be there speaking a certain language, telling a certain story, witnessing to certain non-negotiable things about humanity and about the context in

which humanity lives. A really secular society would be one where there were no more such spaces left.[15]

As we live in the midst of the struggles and contradictions of our predominantly urban, secularizing society, urban spirituality must involve the active pursuit and creation of such spaces, initiated by congregations who also recognize the change they need, and need to be part of. Such spaces are vital to our tactics and strategies as we move towards God's new order, offering room for grace to flourish and the possibility of community in new and dynamic incarnations.

# 9

## *Urban possibilities for daydreaming*

### Andrew Walker

⸺•◆•⸺

A definition of the Examen:

> A review of one's general spiritual health can lead to a resolve
> to be more fully human, fully Christian in a particular area of
> life or relationships . . . It is a prayerful reflection on one's rela-
> tionship with God and with others, as a human being created
> in love for love, but in need of the support and encouragement
> of God's presence along the way.[1]

The form of prayer known as the Examen has long been part
of the Christian tradition, but it is currently largely out of
favour. This in spite of the fact that of the many forms of
prayer experienced within our Christian tradition, it is the one
perhaps best suited to a life under pressure. It can be undertaken while travelling, shopping or performing many of the
more mundane tasks of daily living, and it provides a means
whereby those very tasks – and indeed all the events of life –
are integrated into our faith experience of God. Its unpopular-
ity stems, in part, from the cumbersome and off-putting
nature of its traditional usage, which broke the exercise down
into five consecutive stages, and in part from its emphasis on
introspection, which may make its use appear laborious or
selfish. A recent and excellent book, *Sleeping with Bread*,[2] has
begun to change this by simplifying the structure of the Examen
to two questions while preserving much of its essence, making
the whole more memorable and accessible. Thus 'What today
has drawn me closer to God?' and 'What today has taken me

away from God?' This chapter will explore and explain the dynamics of this most rewarding kind of prayer, perhaps encouraging a fresh generation to experience something of its riches for themselves. A practical example taken from the personal experience of a daily commuter is included to illustrate how this kind of prayer may be adapted and utilized.

My own personal journey with the Examen began in the late 1980s. I began by making myself work through each of the classic stages of the prayer. I tried to do this every evening at bedtime, but found that I was too tired to focus properly. When I moved it to the morning, while walking the dogs on Streatham Common, things fell into place. After a while, it felt right to loosen the structure and adapt some of the questions – it is, after all, a means to an end and, as with learning to ride a bicycle, it needs a great deal of conscious commitment before it becomes habitual and easy.

In traditional practice, the Examen has been inextricably linked with the concept of sin, and it continues to be presented in this light in the popular forms of Compline available. Seen simply as an examination of conscience, it can often be reduced to cataloguing transgressions: 'What have I done wrong today?' In his seminal article on the subject, George Ashenbrenner[3] countered this by renaming it the Examen of Consciousness, beginning the process of broadening and deepening its relevance for a fresh generation.

This reflects part of the general shift in theology and spirituality that took place during the twentieth century. So the movement from conscience to consciousness nicely parallels Dietrich Bonhoeffer's shifting of the demand of ethics from the question of 'How can I be or do good?' to the issue of how to explore 'the reality of the reconciliation of God and humanity brought about through the life, death and resurrection of Christ'.[4] A more recent Papal encyclical, *Veritatis Splendor*, similarly articulated morality's context in the nature of the human person and its relationship with God. With the Examen, therefore, we are part of the move from a purely objective morality of action to a properly informed subjective morality of person. The Examen remains interested in the whole area of personal unfreedom – where one is not free within – and inordinate attachments, but resets these in the proper context of the individual's whole relationship with the Incarnate and Risen God – in the language of the parable, shifting the focus back from profligate child to Prodigal Father.

The Examen has often been linked with the process of discernment and decision-making, but it has a more than valid life beyond that. It is as much about a more intimate knowledge of self and God, and about the growing and deepening relationship between the two, as about any particular choice. Writing in the sixth century, John Climacus comments that what God waits for is not so much the right conclusion about any matter as an increased suppleness in allowing ourselves to fall into his hands for him to work in us.[5] This, then, is about reflection that increases responsiveness, not rightness. For the Society of Jesus it is the method of prayer laid down for all members as part of their training, and it is an exercise par excellence for the process of formation, surely an appropriate word for committed Christians everywhere throughout their life.

Its efficacy, however, depends on its frequency as much as its accessibility and breadth. Even as a daily discipline, it may not be sufficient to foster the supple awareness and sensitivity that is sought. There is a memorable story of Ignatius himself, for whom the Examen was 'central and quite inviolate': he used the Examen hourly. Meeting a Jesuit priest at some point while the day was still far from over, Ignatius asked him how many times he had made the Examen that day. 'Seven times,' the priest answered. 'So few?' was apparently Ignatius's reply.[6]

In the light of all this, an exploration of the dynamic of the Examen would seem timely. Additionally, there is much from the discipline of psychology that can illuminate our current

Christian practice and understanding. Moreover, we seem to
live in an age when the need to adapt and make accessible is
paramount. Hence the advantage of coming to understand, in
depth, a form of prayer that seems so suitable to the demands
and pressures of urban life, all the while exploring an appropriate form for our own personal use and respecting the key to
spiritual practice, which Joe Veale so memorably described as
the 'contemplative grasp of the end and a flexible use of the
means'.[7]

## Consciousness and unconsciousness

Although the Examen is an Examen of Consciousness, the
unconscious certainly influences what happens when people
make it. There are many different ways of expressing the
unconscious, and I will be drawing from the transpersonal
psychologies, particularly psychosynthesis, because they have
most resonances with our Christian faith perspective, and their
insights will be of most use for the purposes of this exploration.

The tendency to dualism, here seen in the need to separate
sacred and secular, dogs any exploration of unconscious
material, and this is true of the early years of the development
of psychosynthesis theory as well as of the tendencies of
general Christian enquiry. Those training on Spiritual Direction programmes ask for ever-greater clarity concerning the
difference between psychology and spirituality, and so between
counselling/therapy and their work. Sometimes, clergy retreat-
ants can see questions about feelings or the past as intrusive
and inappropriate to their ministry. Yet the unconscious has
long been seen as a place of integration, as well as the place
where unwanted thoughts, feelings and events are stored. It
is a place where moral presuppositions, tidy divisions and
detailed cognitive maps are not automatically applicable.

Jung observed that the archetype of wholeness occupies a
central position in the unconscious, and that in the mystery of

the unconscious it is impossible to separate the psychological from the spiritual, should this even be desirable.[8] William Johnston suggests that the mystical path that is open to all is the inner and downward journey to the core of the personality, where the mystery of God and the unity and integrity of creation can also be encountered. Thomas Merton complements this view when he speaks of the overwhelming but (in his day) almost totally neglected importance of exploring our unconsciousness, not just for reasons of personal fulfilment but for its social, theological and communal advantages.

This, then, is the realm of our psyche that lies deeper than our physical, mental and emotional realms, distinct but not entirely separate from them. It is like some great underground river, at times flowing peaceably, at times a torrent, that can provide both life-giving water and life-enhancing power. Its effects are felt both positively and negatively, and can be harnessed creatively – though the prudent will always use caution. Always capable of huge destructive powers, it is also a place of unbelievable richness and potential for our incarnation.

Clearly, some distinctions are necessary if we are to talk of the value of unconscious material, and of how the process of making this material conscious enriches us. Roberto Assagioli, the inspiration behind psychosynthesis, suggests three levels of unconsciousness:[9] the middle is the most accessible and near to consciousness, surrounding what he called the field of consciousness itself; the lower contains the more 'animal', instinctual or darker material; the higher contains unrealized potential and other more positive, though still repressed or suppressed, material. As we have said, though, tidy divisions and moral labels rarely work in this realm. So-called positive qualities can be feared by our conscious self (thus Nelson Mandela's famous speech suggesting that it is our greatness that we fear) and so-called negative emotions, properly explored, can carry great gifts (for example, the self-value and self-assertion that may lie at the heart of unexpressed rage or anger). Higher and lower unconscious material are always intimately connected, and cannot be worked with in isolation. Many therapists working with childhood trauma witness a birth of freedom or a rediscovery of hope or meaning in their clients. Many a spiritual director whose mutual exploration of the faith journey with the directee begins to evoke some darker and more uncomfortable emotions can testify to this as well.

When material from the higher or lower levels comes into consciousness, our freedom is expanded and our minds and hearts become more aware and supple. The conscious part of ourselves has limited capacity and, as our attention is brought to bear on other material, so the previous matter returns to unconsciousness. This time, though, it is neither suppressed nor repressed beyond reach, but is lodged accessibly at the edges of the field of consciousness in the 'middle unconscious'. The role of the Examen in gently allowing unconscious material to be negotiated is thus as a befriender of estranged elements or parts of ourselves, allowing them to be reintegrated.

There are obviously questions to be clarified here about the meaning of 'consciousness'. Again, this is not an area of agreement, particularly about what it is that is aware, or observes, or is conscious within. It seems, certainly, that this is a multi-stranded experience. The first strand could be articulated as an animal awareness, the neural representation of the world that all animals orient themselves by, and to which they behaviourally adjust. The second is possessed only by humans: it consists of the reflective technique, whose operational tool is language.[10] This sets us apart from the rest of creation. On the one hand is simple consciousness or knowing; on the other is the more complex awareness whereby we know that we know. This introduces the question of what it is that knows or is aware, as when we have the sensation of saying something, together with the superimposed feeling that we are saying it.

The experience of consciousness is therefore one of oscillation between instinctual awareness and reflectivity, between reflection and articulation, and between the content of consciousness and the part that seems to be aware. Managing oscillations is an important part of all reflective techniques, from psychosynthesis's Evening Review to, of course, the Examen itself.

## The leader of the band

Psychosynthesis names the part that is aware the self, or I,[11] and proffers the analogy of a conductor of our personal orchestras. The instruments are all that makes up the content of our experience: conscious and unconscious, body, mind, feelings, the different parts of ourselves, the roles we have taken on board and so on. The self has the role of awareness and co-ordination, though its success in this depends on its strength, skill and motivation. The Christian may well be reaching for the word soul at this point, and with justification. The self/soul comprises, above all, the qualities of love and will, and is linked organically to the Higher or Transpersonal Self. Indeed, the language often used to explain this link is identical to the medieval conception of the link between the soul and God: the candle compared to the sun.

This self/soul needs to be nurtured and shaped, as it is always in the process of being formed and strengthened; its ability to be aware needs refining, its skill in co-ordination and integration needs fostering. This is vital, as the self/soul has the task of being a co-creator. As God, in one account of creation at least, broods over the waters and sets about the task of ordering and bringing forth, so the self/soul is confronted with the unconscious elements within its own personality – and with the mess and muddle of daily living and human interaction – and needs to respond to the call similarly to order and bring forth. Thus, interior entropy is reduced as this prayer harmonizes, explores and reconciles through its different elements, which we now explore in turn. What was traditionally

treated as five consecutive stages may more usefully be seen as
five ingredients which together define and make possible the
whole experience, however practically the exercise is used and
adapted by each individual. The following illustration is taken
from the experience of someone I have accompanied in recent
years.

## *The ingredients of the task*

### Celebrating the present moment

> Two days a week I can take the bus straight to the office, the
> rest of the time it's the tube – but the pattern is the same. As I
> leave the house, checking the water level in the cat's bowl and
> that the windows are all locked, I remind myself that God is
> there with me, and I invite him to join with me on the way. The
> streets are usually filthy near my house and there's no green,
> but somehow the fact that we walk together lifts my spirit and
> makes me see things differently. There's always something to
> see, notice or have pointed out; there can even be a kind of
> beauty in things I would otherwise dismiss as ugly.

At the beginning of the Examen, we focus, in gratitude and in
the presence of our God, on the present. We make a statement
about the giftedness of the now, and so stand against that
common tendency to avoid present reality by focusing on the
past (letting ourselves be distracted by memories or by nostal-
gia), looking to the future (occupied by hopes and fears that
present attention will do nothing to change) or making com-
parisons with other people or current situations ('If only it
were different').

The past and future have value, of course, but only in as
much as they impinge usefully on the here and now. Indeed,
they are also present, but not always consciously so. This is
memorably articulated by the novelist Bernhard Schlink:[12]

If something hurts me, the hurts I suffered back then come back to me, and when I feel guilty, the feelings of guilt return; if I yearn for something today, or feel homesick, I feel the yearnings and homesickness from back then. The geological layers of our lives rest so tightly one on top of the other that we always come up against earlier events in later ones, not as matter that has been fully formed and pushed aside, but absolutely present and alive.

Sometimes an encounter or event will trigger past unresolved material; at other times material will come into awareness more gently. Either way, we need to trust ourselves, the present and God as we begin this exercise. The gratitude expressed is a sign of the giftedness of time – time is a gift, for which we are thankful – and of the truth that lies beneath the surface of things; it is also an offering to the giver of the gift. Our self/ soul holds the conductor's baton: we can begin to pay attention to the music.

## Articulating desire and disposition

By the time we've reached the bus stop or platform I am ready to think about the day and what it is I really want from it. Not just getting through it, successfully juggling the emails, calls and meetings while fitting numerous errands and some shopping. But how do I want to be – even who do I want to be? Can I be open to learning and growth? And sometimes the answer, I have to admit, is no – I can't at times cope with any more awareness or choice or freedom, I just want to get by. But I have learnt that that too is okay, God accepts me even then – and patiently waits for the next time. And if that's the case, I only doze for the rest of the journey and have a double espresso when I arrive!

As we gift ourselves a moment set apart from the pressures and distractions of the day, the noise and bustle of our urban environment, we establish the priority of uncovering meaning and increased understanding, and we pray for enlightenment. This is both a duty and a joy, a felt want and an inclination to which we commit ourselves. Making a habit of this will ensure that the practice endures, even when desire or disposition seems absent or weak.

Anthony Storr writes: 'There can be little doubt that humanity is so constituted that we are compelled to seek symbolic solutions and syntheses, and that this trait originated in an adaptive device which better fitted us to master the world in which we found ourselves.'[13]

## Reviewing

> So we trundle along, God and I; there's rarely a seat and so we stand, shoulders in, head down, bag between my feet. But this is the bit I like best – thinking through the day before, or the weekend if it's a Monday morning. It's like the wardrobe in the Narnia stories – I am discreet and faceless on the outside, but inside I journey into another world, going back in time, reliving it, seeing things I missed the first time. There's a chance to put some things right, to enjoy others more fully. Sometimes I even rearrange things a bit – situations, encounters – and see if that would have been better. It's a real adventure.

This third stage is at the heart of the Examen. It is a process of reviewing the events, occurrences, encounters and experiences of whatever period of time has been chosen, of giving an account. As a result, all the associated feelings, connections, thoughts and deeper feelings become clearer. Awareness of themes and patterns, ongoing motives and interests emerge, often over time, as the practice of reflection is sustained, and as we become more sensitive to both the positive and negative forces that lie beneath the surface of things – and to how the Holy Spirit works with us through them both.

In one expression of the developmental stages of the self/soul, David Levin[14] writes of the movement through hearing, to discrimination of hearing, to skilful hearing and to hearkening.

In the regular review of our day, we find a parallel process of increasing discrimination and skill in our seeing as well as our hearing, as we reflect on the time just past. This brings us to a place of listening and seeing with diminished ego and greater sensitivity to how things might be from a divine perspective, thus further liberating our potential as human beings in relation to God.

A variation of this review by restricting and therefore sharpening the focus to current individual needs is contained in many traditions, psychosynthesis included. What is called the Particular Examen in the Spiritual Exercises is the Ignatian version of this. One director of mine, some years ago, took into account an overly self-critical streak and asked me to replace, until further notice, the more general review of the day with the question 'What three things have I done today that God might want to be grateful to me for?' – a nice example of the Ignatian principle of going against particular tendencies to increase freedom, a contemporary version of the Particular Examen, and an example of the Examen's flexibility and adaptability.

Whatever form it takes, this review allows congruence and consonance to come to the surface, as well as any interior dissonance, agitation or disturbance. It is the heart of the whole exercise.

## Releasing sorrow and joy

> We get off and I make my way to my destination. Usually, because of the places I have to visit for work, it's cleaner and greener than where I live and I let that symbolize for me the shedding of all I want now to let go of – whether it's letting myself get caught up in petty politics or snide comments, inappropriate thoughts and actions, or succumbing to simple mindless distraction. And it speaks to me too of a better life, of the ever-real chance for renewal, and that there is always something somewhere to celebrate or give thanks for. Either way I feel freer and my step is usually lighter as I turn the last corner.

We then come to the crucial expression of what the review has touched in us. These are the feelings that have been evoked as a result of insights and increased levels of awareness, a surge of energy that often accompanies the birth of unconscious material into consciousness, for energy has been invested in the matter stored and utilized in keeping it stored. As in child-birth, this can be messy and painful, but if pain, guilt and sorrow are evoked, they will be against a background of thanksgiving and hope. These feelings are then expressed, and so released. The accompanying insights and fruits are taken on board by the soul/self and used; the rest, simple waste or anything 'toxic', will be dispersed. Expression is a way to cleanse and purge.

## Orientation and integration

> As we go through the doors and up in the lift, I spend the last few moments preparing the day ahead and what is most immediately to be done. I know I am going to be preoccupied and that I'll lose touch with much of the peace I have found during my journey – but somehow the fact that it was there as part of my experience makes a difference: I may forget God but he doesn't seem to forget me. I keep meaning to go back to all this at points during the day but that never seems to happen. When I retire perhaps?

The concluding period at the end of the reflective time is crucial for grounding the whole experience, and is integral to this vivifying process – 'vivifying' being a reference to the fact that it 'offers a fuller sense of being alive from moment to moment and this is worth the frequent pain of deeper self awareness'.[15]

At times, this grounding may take the form of a resolution to amend an aspect of life or to commit to a course of behaviour or action, but it is always part of turning our attention outwards and to the future. Our coming more to life is in order to help others live; our time of reflection is in the service of our time of action, and the further exploration of our identity facilitates our choices and our building of the Kingdom in, and through, all of who we are and what we do.

# Daydreaming

Dreams have always been centrally important in the exploration of the unconscious. But Freud's 'royal road to the unconscious', as he referred to dreams, was a road to a dark and pessimistic place. Jung's interpretation of what he called the Shadow was much more positive, a place that was 'ninety-nine per cent pure gold', and this understanding has been taken up and developed by psychosynthesis.

As well as dreams, daydreams have always played their part in exploring the unconscious and in allowing all kinds of material to come into awareness and be accepted. This approach was pioneered in the middle of the twentieth century by Robert Desoille, in his concept of the waking dream.[16] In it, the patient is guided through an imaginative journey of descent and ascent, itself based on Dante's *Divine Comedy*, but using the individual's own unconscious material. This approach, which as a technique is both diagnostic and therapeutic, is still used in adapted form by psychosynthesis practitioners today.

The movement of descent and ascent relates both in space and time to our use of the Examen – we move back through a reflection of the day, or period of time, and re-emerge into the present informed and enhanced by greater awareness and insight. At the same time, we delve beneath the surface of thoughts, feelings and events into the unconscious truths and treasures that are buried within, bringing back into consciousness the gold we have discovered. It is, above all, the movement of Holy Saturday and the harrowing of hell – the bringing of the gospel to the darkest corners of creation and the bringing of that darkness into the light. The reflectivity of this kind of daydream can thus be both radical and redemptive.

## *Conclusion*

For Dietrich Bonhoeffer, the strictly ethical life needed always to be relativized; but even when, faced with ambiguous circumstances, we have to make difficult decisions, our life is 'wonderfully enfolded by good powers'.[17] Hence, we can always move forward in trust and hope, whether in the chaos Bonhoeffer faced in 1945 or in the ambiguous and difficult situations we face today, exacerbated by the urban realities of noise, grime, overcrowding and the ever-present threat of violence or terrorism.

There will always be those who will continue to condemn introspection, who therefore remain uneasy with the insights of psychology and avoid the Examen and similar prayer exercises. But introspection undertaken in faith grounds our human experience in those good powers of God, and can radically transform our perspective. As Harry Williams reminds us: 'Theological enquiry is basically related to self-awareness and therefore it involves a process of self-discovery so that, whatever else theology is, it must in some sense be a theology of the self'.[18]

Given that Christianity proclaims a God whose own self is irrevocably committed to the human, we cannot make a sharp distinction between what is human and what is divine. What we say about God will always have immediate and personal implications for our lives; our reflection on ourselves and on how we have spent our time will always have relevance to our understanding of God.

As a form of prayer, the Examen is infinitely adaptable, whether one uses the five ingredients mentioned above in a formal five-part time of prayer, adapting the enquiry to a particular circumstance, or whether one engages with those same ingredients in the two-question format suggested in *Sleeping with Bread*. Above all, it is a reflection that requires no additional time or commitment, other than the discipline of regular attention given – whether on the bus or Tube, at the sink or at the photocopier, queuing at the supermarket, while walking the dog or travelling to collect the children from school – at whatever point of the day may be convenient.

I believe this form of prayer is unsurpassed as a means of allowing God's word, spoken in and through the complexities of modern living, to be heard. This faith version of daydreaming ensures an opportunity to reflect on our lives in a creative and redemptive way, increasing our sensitivity to the ways of our God and to all that will build his Kingdom in our lives and in our world. It also permits that crucial space for the Holy Spirit to surprise us daily as our spiritual journey unfolds. Its power to provide a gateway to unconscious material and a gentle means whereby that material can be usefully transformed is also crucial to our development as human beings under God. Both theology and the transpersonal psychologies stand for an integrated humanity, one that recognizes the reality of our transpersonal or divine potential; both support this ancient spiritual practice of examining our lives. For Dietrich Bonhoeffer, freedom existed in courageously grasping reality; in the Examen, this is at the heart of what we do, all the while being reminded that we remain, both individually and communally, wonderfully enfolded by God.

# Notes

## 1 Reclaiming faith

1 Graham Ward, *Cities of God*. London: Routledge, 2000, p. 33.
2 Ward, p. 28.
3 Italo Calvino, *The Literature Machine* (trans. Patrick Creagh). London: Picador, 1989, pp. 17–18.
4 Grace Davie, *Religion in Britain since 1945: Believing without Belonging*. Oxford: Blackwell, 1994.
5 Steve Bruce, *From Cathedrals to Cults: Religion in the Modern World*. Oxford: OUP, 1996, p. 230.
6 Jacques Ellul, *Living Faith: Belief and Doubt in a Perilous World* (trans. Peter Heinegg). San Francisco: Harper & Row, 1983.
7 Evelyn Underhill, *Essential Writings* (ed. Emilie Griffin). Maryknoll, NY: Orbis, 2003, p. 26.
8 Yann Martel, *The Life of Pi*. Edinburgh: Canongate, 2002.
9 Underhill, p. 31.
10 Cited in Yves M.-J. Congar, *The Mystery of the Temple* (trans. Reginald F. Trevett). London: Burns & Oates, 1962, p. 197.
11 Diarmaid MacCulloch, *Reformation: Europe's Houses Divided 1490–1700*. London: Allen Lane, 2003, p. 3.
12 John Gray, *Heresies*. London: Granta, 2004, p. 17.
13 Karen Armstrong, *The Spiral Staircase: A Memoir*. London: Harper Perennial, 2005, p. 3.

## 2 Urbanization, the Christian Church and the human project

1 Bishop Challoner, *The Garden of the Soul: A Manual of Spiritual Exercises and Instructions for Christians Who, Living in the World, Aspire to Devotion*. London: Burns & Oates, 1740.
2 Sam Wells, *Community-Led Regeneration and the Local Church*. Cambridge: Grove Booklets, 2003.
3 Andrew Shanks, *God and Modernity*. London: Routledge, 2000, pp. 29–33.

## 3 Hymns and the city

1 See Rosalind Brown, *How Hymns Shape Our Lives*. Cambridge: Grove, 2001.

2 For example, Jacques Ellul, *The Meaning of the City*. Grand Rapids, MI: Eerdmans, 1993; Graham Ward, *Cities of God*. London: Routledge, 2000. See also, for example, Isaiah 1.21, Nahum 3.1.

3 Rod Garner, *Facing the City*. Peterborough: Epworth Press, 2004. See also, for example, Psalm 122.3, Zechariah 8.3–8.

4 For example, Harvey Cox, *The Secular City*. London: Penguin, 1965. See the critique in Garner, *Facing the City*, p. 102.

5 'Judge eternal, throned in splendour', by Henry Scott Holland (1847–1918).

6 'King of the City Splendid', by George Thomas Coster (1835–1912).

7 'England arise!', by Edward Carpenter (1844–1929).

8 Percy Dearmer (ed.), *Songs of Praise Discussed*. London: OUP, 1965, p. 178.

9 'When cross the crowded ways of life', by Frank Mason North (1850–1935).

10 'The founders built this city', by William Tarrant (1853–1928).

11 'When through the whirl of wheels, and engines humming', by Geoffrey Studdart-Kennedy (1883–1929).

12 'God of the pastures, hear our prayer', by T. C. Hunter Clarke (1910–1984).

13 'Come let us remember the joys of the town', by Doris Gill (published in 1951).

14 'God of concrete, God of steel', by R. C. Jones (b. 1926).

15 'When the bells chime noon in London', by Paul Townsend (b. 1923).

16 'A cry in the night', by Geoffrey Ainger (b. 1925).

17 'We meet you, O Christ, in many a guise', by Fred Kaan (b. 1929) and 'We have a dream, we have a dream', by Martin Eggleton (b. 1938).

18 'Sing we a song of high revolt', by Fred Kaan (b. 1929).

19 'Jesus Christ is waiting, waiting in the streets', by John Bell (b. 1949) and Graham Moule (b. 1958).

20 'City of man, how rich and right', by Fred Kaan (b. 1929).

21 This hymn book came soon after, and embodies the view expressed on page 70 of the Church of England report, *Faith in the
City*. London: Church House Publishing, 1985. 'We believe that
God, though infinitely transcendent, is also to be found, despite
all appearances, in the apparent waste lands of our inner cities
and housing estates . . . that the city is not to be shunned as a
concentration of evil but enjoyed as a unique opportunity for
human community.'

22 *Hymns of the City*, Introduction, ed. John Vincent. Sheffield:
Urban Theology Unit, 1998.

23 'Dear God of town and city', by Margaret Mackle (fl. 1989),
reproduced from *Hymns of the City* by permission.

24 'Yours the city, yours the city', by John Vincent (fl. 1989) © John
Vincent, reproduced from *Hymns of the City* by permission.

25 Matthew 8.20.

26 See Laurie Green, 'Blowing Bubbles: Poplar' in Peter Sedgwick
(ed.), *God in the City*. London: Mowbray, 1995, pp. 77–9 for a
discussion of the sense of sin that inner city residents experience,
and thus bring to worship.

27 'O Lord, the clouds are gathering', by Graham Kendrick (b. 1950).

28 'Desolate cities, desolate homes', by Graham Kendrick (b. 1950).

29 'Beauty for brokenness', by Graham Kendrick (b. 1950).

30 'O worship the Lord in the beauty of holiness', by John S. B.
Mounsell (1811–1875).

31 'O little town of Bethlehem', by Phillips Brooks (1835–1893).

## 4  Living in knowable communities

1 Thomas Hardy, *Journal*, 28 March 1888.

2 1995 BBC Reith Lectures.

3 *Dombey and Son*, Chapter 47.

4 A. Mearns and W. C. Preston, *The Bitter Cry of Outcast London*.
London: James Clarke, 1883.

5 Peter Townsend, *Poverty and Labour in London*. London: Low
Pay Unit, 1987.

6 David Sheppard, *Built as a City: God and the Urban World
Today*. London: Hodder & Stoughton, 1974.

7 Church of England. Archbishop of Canterbury's Commission on
Urban Priority Areas, *Faith in the City: A Call for Action by Church
and Nation*. London: Church House, 1985.

8  Anthony Harvey (ed.), *Theology in the City*. London: SPCK, 1989.
9  'A Vision for London', *Christian Action Journal*, Autumn 1990.

## 5  Bearing it: the development of a priestly spirituality in Soho

1  L. William Countryman, *Living on the Border of the Holy: Renewing the Priesthood of All*. Harrisburg, PA: Morehouse Publishing, 1999, p. 21.
2  Penny Jamieson, *Living at the Edge*. London: Mowbray, 1997, p. 4.

## 6  Cities and human community

1  These figures are cited by Sir Crispin Tickell in his Introduction to Richard Rogers, *Cities for a Small Planet*. London: Faber & Faber, 1997, p. 7.
2  See, for example, the comments of Anne Buttimer in 'Home, Reach and the Sense of Place' in Anne Buttimer and David Seamon (eds), *The Human Experience of Space and Place*. London: Croom Helm, 1980.
3  Buttimer, p. 174.
4  Arnold Berleant, *The Aesthetics of Environment*. Philadelphia: Temple University Press, 1992, pp. 86–7.
5  Marc Augé, *Non-Places: Introduction to an Anthropology of Supermodernity*. London/New York: Verso, 1997, especially pp. 51–2 and p. 77.
6  Richard Sennett, *The Conscience of the Eye: The Design and Social Life of Cities*. London: Faber & Faber, 1993, p. xii.
7  Sennett, pp. xii–xiii.
8  Sennett, pp. 6–10.
9  Sennett, pp. 10–19.
10  See John S. Dunne, *The City of the Gods: A Study in Myth and Mortality*. London: Sheldon Press, 1974, ch. 7, 'The City of God', particularly p. 158.
11  This is the emphasis of Augustine's commentary on Genesis and is cited in Robert Markus, *The End of Ancient Christianity*. Cambridge: Cambridge University Press, 1990, p. 78.
12  On the development of medieval cities, see Jacques Le Goff, *Medieval Civilisation*. Oxford: Blackwell, 1988, pp. 70–8.

13 See Peter Raedts, 'The Medieval City as a Holy Place' in Charles Caspers and Marc Schneiders (eds), *Omnes Circumadstantes: Contributions towards a History of the Role of the People in the Liturgy*. Kampen: Uitgeversmaatschappij J. H. Kok, 1990, pp. 144–54.

14 For interesting remarks on the relationship between the fragmentation of intellectual discourse, starting with the medieval separation of theology and spirituality, and the contemporary secularization of the city, see James Matthew Ashley, *Interruptions: Mysticism, Politics and Theology in the work of Johann Baptist Metz*. Notre Dame, IA: University of Notre Dame Press, 1998, pp. 10–12.

15 See Berleant, p. 62.

16 Augé, p. 66.

17 Augé, pp. 66–7.

18 Michel de Certeau, 'Walking in the City', in his *The Practice of Everyday Life*. Berkeley: University of California Press, 1988, pp. 91–110.

19 De Certeau, 'Walking in the City', p. 92.

20 De Certeau, 'Walking in the City', p. 96.

21 De Certeau, 'Indeterminate', in *The Practice of Everyday Life*, p. 203.

22 De Certeau, *The Practice of Everyday Life*, p. 115.

23 De Certeau, *The Practice of Everyday Life*, pp. 122–30.

24 Franco LaCecia, 'The space of play'. Royal Society of Arts, 1999.

25 See also the essay by Michael Northcott, 'Children', in Peter Sedgwick (ed.), *God in the City*. London: Mowbray, 1995, pp. 139–52.

26 LaCecia.

27 It is disturbing that one of the largest, and apparently most comprehensive and interdisciplinary modern books on the city, has no explicit reference at all to ethical or 'spiritual' perspectives and scarcely mentions religion except in terms of archaeology. This is explained by the surprising philosophical lacunae – no translations of continental thinkers, no references at all to figures such as de Certeau, Foucault or Augé and only footnote citations of Lefebvre. See Richard T. LeGates and Frederic Stout (eds), *The City Reader*. London: Routledge, 1999.

28 See Richard Rogers, *Cities for a Small Planet*. London: Faber & Faber, 1997, p. 19.

29 Rogers, pp. 167–8.
30 Charles Leadbeater, *Civic Spirit: The Big Idea for a New Political Era*. Demos Arguments 14. London: Demos, 1997.
31 Leadbeater, p. 30.
32 Haddon Wilmer, 'Images of the City and the Shaping of Humanity' in Anthony Harvey (ed.), *Theology in The City*. London: SPCK, 1989, p. 37.
33 'Baptism, Eucharist and Ministry, Faith and Order Paper 111'. Geneva: WCC, 1982, para. 19–20 and 22.

## 7 Urban spirituality: one size does not fit all

1 S. Bevans, *Models of Contextual Theology*. Faith and Culture Series. Rev. edn Maryknoll, NY: Orbis, 2002.
2 Trans. Sr Kathleen England, *In the Heart of the City, In the Heart of God: Jerusalem Community Rule of Life*. Manila: St Paul's, 1994, p. 94.
3 Wisdom 9.8; Nehemiah 11.1; Baruch 4.30–36; Zechariah 8.3; Lamentations 2.15; Isaiah 35.10, 52.1; Jeremiah 30.18; Ezekiel 36.35; Luke 13.33; John 7.15; Mark 14.13; Acts 1.3; Acts 2; Revelation 21.2–3, 23. There is no acknowledgement in the Rule of the community of the ambiguity of the city symbol in Scripture as is evident when the city is compared to a prostitute who is unfaithful to Yahweh (Isaiah 23.15–18) or Babylon to the mother of harlots (Rev. 17.1–6).
4 In ancient times cities were walled and villages unwalled.
5 *In the Heart of the City*, pp. 91–6.
6 J. Leclercq, 'Urban Monasticism Today: Why?', *Word and Spirit: A Monastic Review. No 16, The Monastery and the City*. Petersham, MS: St Bede's Publications, 1979, pp. 70–81.
7 R. Poleman, 'Une vocation d'érmite', *Vie consacrée* 48, 1976, pp. 341–51.
8 The name 'Sojourner' was not attached to the community until 1975, when the community moved from Chicago to Washington.
9 J. Wallis, *Revive Us Again: A Sojourner's Story*. Nashville, TN: Abingdon Press, 1983, p. 4.
10 K. Lattea, 'The Paradox of City Life', *Sojourners* 24/3, 1995, p. 41.
11 Bevans, p. 88.
12 M. Eastman, 'Faith in the City: A Review Article', *Urban Mission* 4/3, 1987, pp. 6–15.

13 A. Smith, *Passion for the Inner City*. London: Sheed & Ward, 1983.

14 C. Marchant, B. Reed, A. Smith, 'Faith in the City', *Modern Churchman* 28/2, 1986, pp. 3–10.

15 Archbishop of Canterbury's Commission on Urban Priority Areas, *Faith in the City: A Call for Action by Church and Nation*. London: Church House Publishing, 1985, p. iii.

16 *Faith in the City*, p. 360.

17 C. Marchant, *Signs in the City*. London: Hodder & Stoughton, 1985. This work was followed by another which specifically aims to illustrate how to build on the signs of hope in the city: Marchant, *Shalom My Friends: Building God's Kingdom Together*. Basingstoke: Marshall Pickering, 1988. A similar style of reflection is pursued in L. Green, *God in the Inner City: Christian Religious Experience in the Urban Environment*. New City Special, 10. Sheffield: Urban Theology Unit, 1993.

18 G. Goulding, *On the Edge of Mystery: Towards a Spiritual Hermeneutic of the Urban Margins*. Religions and Discourse, vol. 8. Oxford: Peter Lang, 2000.

19 Marchant, *Signs in the City*, p. 15.

20 *Signs in the City*, pp. 50–65.

21 Approaching the city as a repository of signs of hope informed the edition of *Christian Ministry* which reflected on 'Urban Ministry Today': *Christian Ministry*, 20/2, 1989.

22 The hope for inner cities in the emergence of small Christian communities is also described in H. C. Conn, ' "Any Faith Dies in the City" – The Secularization Myth', *Urban Mission* 3/5, 1986, pp. 6–19.

23 M. Walsh, *Here's Hoping: Heath Town, Wolverhampton, and the Hope Community*. New City Special, 8. Sheffield: Urban Theology Unit, 1991.

24 Goulding, p. 59.

25 J. Vincent, 'An Urban Hearing for the Gospel', in C. Rowland, J. Vincent (eds), *Gospel from the City*. British Liberation Theology, 2. Sheffield: Urban Theology Unit, 1997, pp. 105–16.

26 See M. O'Sullivan, 'The Human Spirit and the Option for the Economically Poor', in B. Flanagan and D. Kelly (eds), *Lamplighters: Exploring Spirituality in New Contexts*. Dublin: Veritas, 2004, pp. 62–72.

27 Bevans, p. 103.
28 B. Flanagan, *The Spirit of the City: Voices from Dublin's Liberties.* Dublin: Veritas, 1999.
29 Flanagan, *Spirit of the City*, p. 199.
30 L. Russell, 'The City as Battered Woman', *The Other Side* 24, May 1988, pp. 20–1.
31 S. Hauerwas, *A Community of Character: Toward a Constructive Christian Social Ethic.* Notre Dame, IN: University of Notre Dame Press, 1981, p. 74.
32 S. Hauerwas, W. William, *Resident Aliens.* Nashville, TN: Abingdon Press, 1989, p. 30.
33 Hauerwas, *A Community of Character*, p. 80.
34 R. Siebert, 'Urbanization as a World Trend: A Challenge to the Churches', *Missiology* 13, 1985, pp. 429–43.
35 John Paul II, *Centesimus Annus*, para. 33.
36 John Paul II, 'Renew Dimensions of Lay and Ecclesial Life: Address to the Representatives of National Catholic Organisations in Brazil', 29 January 1979, in *Servant of Truth: Messages of John Paul II.* Boston, MA: Daughters of Saint Paul, 1979, pp. 284–8.
37 John Paul II, 'Renew', 'Les situations nouvelles sont le terreau de l'évangélisation: Allocution aux évêques français de la Région "Nord"', in *La documentation catholique* 2097845, 1992, pp. 204–6.

## 8 The spirituality of everyday life

1 Stephen Sykes, 'Spirituality and Mental Sickness', in Mark Theissen Nation and Samuel Wells, *Faithfulness and Fortitude: In Conversation with the Theological Ethics of Stanley Hauerwas.* Edinburgh: T & T Clark, 2000, pp. 71–2.
2 Psalm 48.11–12.
3 See Gustavo Gutiérrez, *The Destiny of the Present. Selected Writings.* Maryknoll, NY: Orbis Books, 1999, pp. 150–3.
4 See Philip Sheldrake's comments on Egeria's encounters with the ascetics of fourth-century Palestine in *Spaces for the Sacred.* London: SCM Press, 2001, p. 39.
5 Leonie Sandercock, *Towards Cosmopolis.* Chichester: John Wiley, 1998, p. 219.

6 See Andrew Davey, *Urban Christianity and Global Order: Theological Resources for an Urban Future*. London: SPCK, 2001, pp. 53–5.

7 See Michel de Certeau *et al.*, *The Practice of Everyday Life*. Volume 2: Living and Cooking, Minnesota: University of Minnesota Press, 1998, pp. 7–13.

8 Richard Sennett, *Conscience of the Eye. The Design and Social Life of Cities*. London: Faber, 1990, p. 123.

9 Henri Lefebvre, *Writing on Cities*, ed. and trans. by Elenore Kofman and Elizabeth Lebas. Oxford: Blackwell, 1996, pp. 147–59.

10 Michel de Certeau, *The Practice of Everyday Life*. Berkeley: University of California Press, 1984, pp. xviii–xx.

11 Theodore Eastman, 'Mission of Christ in Urban America', in Philip Turner and Frank Sugeno, *Crossroads Are for Meeting*. Sewanee, TN: SPCK/USA, 1986, p. 228.

12 Davey, pp. 105–7.

13 Arthur Vogel, *Radical Christianity and the Flesh of Jesus*. London: DLT, 1996, p. 124.

14 Stephen Sykes, *Unashamed Anglicanism*. London: DLT, 1995, p. 203.

15 Dimbleby Lecture available at: <http://www.archbishopof canterbury.org/sermons_speeches/021219.html>

# 9 Urban possibilities for daydreaming

1 *The New Dictionary of Catholic Spirituality*. Collegeville, MN: Liturgical Press, 1993, p. 364.

2 Sheila Dennis and Matthew Linn, *Sleeping with Bread: Holding what Gives You Life*. Mahwah, NJ: Paulist Press, 1995.

3 George Ashenbrenner, *Review for Religious*, vol. 31, 1972, St Louis, MO.

4 Dietrich Bonhoeffer, *Collected Works*, vol. 6, London: SCM Press, 1993.

5 Colm Luibheid and Benedicta Ward (trans.), *The Ladder of Divine Ascent*. London: SPCK, 1982, p. 244.

6 R. Bautista sj, *Hearts Burning*. Philippines: Bookmark, 1990, p. 34.

7 Joe Veale, *Way Supplement* 48, Autumn 1983, Heythrop, London, p. 20.

8 I am indebted for the following three quotes to Judith Reger ssj and her article 'Dreams in the Spiritual Life', from *Human Development*, vol. 18, 3, Fall 1997, Chicago, IL.

9 Roberto Assagioli, *Psychosynthesis: A Manual of Principles and Techniques*. London: Aquarian Press/Thorsons, 1993, p. 17.

10 I have drawn heavily on the work of Zoltan Torey here and his *Crucible of Consciousness*. London: OUP, 1999, pp. 129f. He would not agree with my conclusions!

11 Piero Ferrucci, *What We May Be*. Wellingborough: Crucible/ Aquarian Press, 1989.

12 Bernhard Schlink, *The Reader* (trans. Carol Brown Janeway). London: Weidenfeld & Nicholson, 1997.

13 Anthony Storr, *The Dynamics of Creation*. Harmondsworth: Pelican, 1976, p. 217.

14 David Levin, *The Listening Self*. London: Routledge, 1989, pp. 46f.

15 Jerome Singer, *Daydreaming and Fantasy*. Oxford: OUP, 1981, p. 261.

16 Robert Desoille, *La Rêve Eveillé en Psychotherapie*. Paris: Presse Universitaires, 1945.

17 This comes from an unpublished poem written by Bonhoeffer in the last year of his life. Its source was Philip Endean, editor of *The Way*, the July 2003 publication of which contained on earlier version of this chapter.

18 Harry Williams, *True Resurrection*. London: Fount, 1983, preface.

The Society for Promoting Christian Knowledge (SPCK) was
founded in 1698. Its mission statement is:

**To promote Christian knowledge by**
- **Communicating the Christian faith in its
  rich diversity;**
- **Helping people to understand the Christian faith
  and to develop their personal faith; and**
- **Equipping Christians for mission and ministry.**

SPCK Worldwide serves the Church through Christian
literature and communication projects in over 100 countries, and
provides books for those training for ministry in many parts of
the developing world. This worldwide service depends upon the
generosity of others and all gifts are spent wholly on ministry
programmes, without deductions.

SPCK Bookshops support the life of the Christian community
by making available a full range of Christian literature and other
resources, providing support for those training for ministry, and
assisting bookstalls and book agents throughout the UK.

SPCK Publishing produces Christian books and resources,
covering a wide range of inspirational, pastoral, practical and
academic subjects. Authors are drawn from many different
Christian traditions, and publications aim to meet the needs of a
wide variety of readers in the UK and throughout the world.

The Society does not necessarily endorse the individual views
contained in its publications, but hopes they stimulate readers to
think about and further develop their Christian faith.

For further information about the Society, visit our website at
*www.spck.org.uk* or write to:
SPCK, 36 Causton Street,
London SW1P 4ST, United Kingdom.